"How can I tell her to stop taking drink and drugs when it's the only thing that blots out the pain?

Some days you just have to **weep with those that weep,** and go from there."

# CONTENTS

Revd. Don Robins' words as written in 1930 describe St George's Crypt as a beacon and a refuge. His words still hold true in modern-day society that 'the tasks that confront us are enormous, but the strength of those who put their trust in God is unlimited.'

We are all God's children, wonderfully and fearfully created in His likeness, each of infinite worth.

To respond in a Christ-like manner to each other and to seek to serve others, is to recognise that there is no 'them' and 'us.'

St George's Crypt reaches out to people who are in need and seeks to support them. Staff at the Crypt offer a wide variety of training and engagement opportunities to those who are most vulnerable, rebuilding lost confidence, self-worth and grow life-skills.

The lives that once were so often unbearably painful find new paths and in this way, restoration of hope and of healing becomes possible.

The Crypt helps us to rediscover our common humanity and work together as members of the one race... the human race.

We see this in Jesus' arms stretched out on the Cross which are for the whole world. He raises our hopes, not to dash them, but to energise us with new life and transforming love.

Please join me in praying for the work of the Crypt.

Let the Lighthouse Church, as set up by the Crypt, shine out the love of God for all.

**The Most Reverend & Right Honourable
Dr. John Sentamu
Archbishop of York**

Although I have lived in Leeds for many years, it was only recently that the Crypt really came to my attention.

My 'real' awareness began over a coffee and scone at Cockpit Farm Tea Rooms near Otley.

St George's Crypt were their nominated charity of the year, and they had some old 'Entertaining Angels' books for sale.

The gritty photography grabbed me straight away, and I bought a copy to read later.

That night at home I read the first few pages... and it moved me so much I finished it in one sitting.

At 2am I shut the book and tried to get some sleep, but with very mixed feelings about charity, homelessness, humanity and my role in their story.

Later that month, I met with Chris Fields and it became apparent that a new 'story' about the Crypt was needed... and the idea behind 'Entertaining More Angels' was born.

We started work on the book in February 2015, and it has been a real partnership with the Crypt, their key partners and the creative talents at Leeds College of Art. Students and staff alike have spent many days interviewing, illustrating, photographing and of course meeting to turn an idea into reality.

All of us hope that you enjoy this latest version of the St George's Crypt story.

Edward Ryder - Biskit Ltd

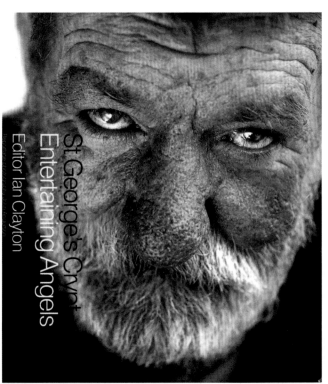

St George's Crypt
Entertaining Angels
Editor Ian Clayton

Entertaining Angels was the first complete book about the crypt. It told a moving story about the origins of the Crypt, through to the late 1990's.

Limited copies are still available from the Crypt.

## Welcome to our second 'Entertaining Angels' book.
## This is a continuation of the 'who, where and why' that was so well documented in the first book.

'Why do a second book?,' some might say.

Surely the issue of homelessness has been tackled by now, and we can focus upon other issues?

Sadly, the answer is no. Although our knowledge and resources have improved dramatically in 85 years, some of the underlying issues surrounding society and homelessness have got worse.

We still need to tell you our current story about how the Crypt, as a beacon of safety, refuge and hope is continuing to deliver immediate need and good counsel with training and preparation for the long term.

Whilst our Christian ethos and practice have not changed, our services certainly have.

As times change, we need to evolve in order to be on the frontline of service delivery, helping the most vulnerable in society.

The need is greater than ever and we now operate a 24/7/365 service, offering a multi-layered and diverse system of support, care and most importantly Christian love.

We really hope that in reading this book you will see that the Crypt has moved onwards and outwards into the community, through our shops, hostels and cafés.

Please help us spread the news that change really is possible. A new life for our clients is difficult, but achievable with the development of skills, training and empowerment.

The need for support within a community, be that in the Crypt or the big wide world, is paramount for a successful transition to a 'normal' life. To that end, and regardless of client circumstance, our community and support work remains at the core of our homelessness strategy.

We will of course always be there for the immediate need of food and shelter, but with the help of our supporters and friends we are able to offer extra hope for the future; the ability to support oneself and fellowship in the love of Christ.

A guest of the Crypt once said 'My future has been cancelled until further notice.'

Not on our watch my friend!

Our strapline is taken straight from the Gospel of Matthew, "I was a stranger and you invited me in."

As true today as ever was and ever will be.

**Chris Fields, CEO,
St George's Crypt**

# HISTORY

St George's Crypt is a direct result of the distressing consequences of the Great Depression on many people in the great city of Leeds and the impact this had on one man... Don Robins.

Don arrived in Leeds in 1930 and was immediately struck by the poverty and destitution he found in his new parish – St George's in central Leeds.

He vowed not to preach another sermon in the pulpit until he did something positive for those at the gate of the church who were increasingly disheartened at the prospect of no work and with very little to feed their families.

He soon discovered that the redundant Crypt of the church, which hadn't been used for 55 years, might be the saving grace for these despairing people.

With the help of parishioners, he opened the gates and cleared away the grime, rubble and bodies in order to open the facility to those in need on 15 October 1930.

Within a short space of time, Don and his faithful team created a workable space where needy people could come and enjoy basic food and fellowship.

In 1955, those coffins which remained in the Crypt were relocated, and at last the building was reclaimed for the living rather than the dead.

The work of Don, which he tirelessly and totally unselfishly offered, was brought to a sudden end in 1948 when he died, aged only 48.

There was a real concern at that time that the work of the Crypt might end with his death.

Fortunately, the Crypt entered a new phase of development when a young enthusiastic clergyman called Tony Waite was appointed. Initially he faced resistance, because much in the Crypt had been built in Don's indomitable style.

However, he soon settled in and brought great gifts to the Crypt, notably when Wilfred Pickles brought his 'Have A Go' team from the BBC.

There had been a policy that no charity would be endorsed by the programme; however Wilfred was so moved by the Crypt that he went against this decision and appealed for support. The results were marvellous.

The Crypt was then led by Don Paterson who further developed work for families and also pioneered the hostel work.

By the late 1990s however, the Crypt required major refurbishment. A massive appeal for £1,450,000, 'More Than A Roof', was launched. While there were a few concerning moments, the appeal was achieved in 1999 and the Crypt that we can see today was born.

It was a tremendous achievement and opened the door to more focused client-based work, and was the start of our training and engagement programme.

In 2009, the Crypt achieved another major milestone when an additional pavilion with training rooms and an extra 12 individual rooms for overnight rough sleepers were added.

The basic work of practical care and support for homeless people remains the cornerstone of the Crypt. The Christian beliefs which run through all the work are as robust now as they were in 1930.

The differences today centre around greatly enhanced opportunities, updated facilities and staff expertise which deliver training and engagement plus a range of life skills programmes for clients.

The core mission in the Crypt is to offer a service which takes a client from access as a rough sleeper, through to readiness to sustain independent living.

None of this would have been possible without the inspiration and vision of Don Robins – there is so much to thank him for!

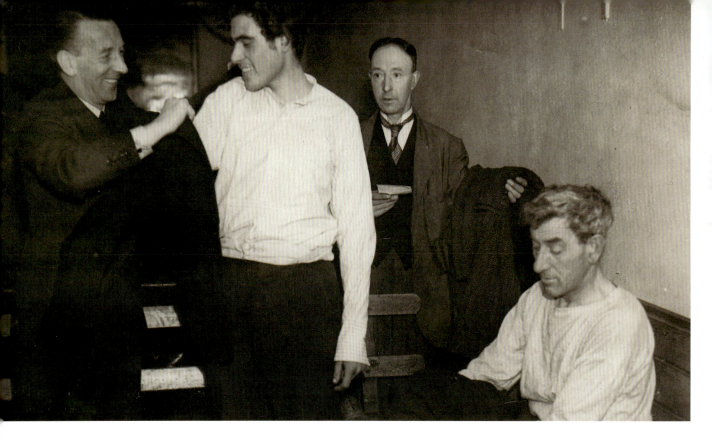

Wilfred Pickles, BBC Entertainer and Presenter of 'Have a Go,' fitting jackets on clients.

Massed crowds at the funeral of Revd. Don Robins.

Revd. Tony Waite, protégé of Revd. Don Robins, unloading the Crypt van.

The founder of the Crypt, Revd. Don Robins, was laid to rest in 1948.

# CHRISTIANITY

Soon after becoming Chaplain to the Crypt in Autumn 2013, I realised that the ordinary Church wasn't speaking to many of our friends here.

I then learned that there had originally been a Crypt service on Sunday afternoons. This seemed like a good idea, but would probably have remained only that, had not Revd. Jon Swales come and asked how I would feel about having a service in the Crypt on Sunday afternoons!

Such 'leading of the Spirit' is a great blessing, which was confirmed when we proposed the concept to Chris Fields. He listened, sat back and smiled, and said I've been praying for this for seven years.

So it was that the 'Lighthouse' began in January 2014. Led by Jon Swales, our services aim to meet people where they are; to come to them rather than demanding that they come to church.

We meet sometime after 12:30 in the Assisi Café of the Crypt, and begin by singing the James Taylor hit 'You've got a friend.' This is another way of seeing holiness in the world, rather than claiming the church has a monopoly on God.

Led by Jon Swales; testimony, prayer, sketches, dancing and singing all find their place in the Lighthouse.

We then share lunch together. Attendance is normally between 40-60, and so enthusiastically has this ministry been received that Jon now runs additional Bible studies and services through the week, together with particular support to those in need.

More than twenty of the flock have been baptised over the past year.

**Revd. Roger Quick, Chaplain to the Homeless**

Humanity, it is said, comes with age when we have grown up, matured and are capable of being masters of our own destiny.

However, as we ponder that thought consider this: we have taller buildings but shorter tempers, we have wider motorways but narrower viewpoints.

We spend more, but have less.

We have more degrees but less common sense.

We have more knowledge but less judgement.

We have more acquaintances but fewer friends.

We live in times of more leisure but have less fun.

We live in fancier houses, but there are more broken homes, less security and more divorce.

We have higher incomes but lower morals.

We have multiplied possessions, but reduced our values.

We have learnt how to make a living, but not how to live life.

It is a time when there is much in the shop window, but nothing in the stock room.

We have been all the way to the moon and back, but cannot cross the street to help a neighbour.

Why, because we have concentrated so much upon ourselves and lost sight of who we are, where we are going and what we are meant to be doing.

**Chris Puckrin.**

CHRISTOPHER BECKETT ESQ<sup>R</sup>. ONE OF THE PRINCIPAL FOVNDERS OF

# Beautiful Beauty Broken Broke

Beauty.  The thing that creates intense pleasure or deep satisfaction.

Beauty in the wrinkles around deep and soulful eyes.  Beauty in the sun-kissed landscape.  Beauty in the moment of connection of two hearts.  Beauty in the moments of massed non-violent protests against injustice.

Beauty.  In the minuscule and the massive.  It's everywhere and it's just out of reach.

Brokenness.  The thing that's left after violation, crushing or forcible separation.

Brokenness in the frail, ageing and dying body.  Brokenness in the scorching and devastation of the rainforest.  Brokenness in the heart of a child who can't understand why their parents hate each other.  Brokenness in the society that allows the 1% to abuse the 99.

Brokenness.  In the minuscule and the massive.  It's everywhere and just beyond cure.

As a society we have a strange relationship with birth and death.  The two most natural of all human passages.  Our society would have us hide them away in whitewashed, clinical, sterile environments.  We take the most human moments and put them in the most inhumane buildings.

Maybe we can't really cope with seeing beauty and brokenness up close and personal.  Maybe there's something in us that is happier to pretend everything is 'ok' rather than face the fact that we're surrounded by astonishing beauty and devastating brokenness.

Maybe the reason we hide behind Facebook profiles, dress ourselves in other people's labels, define ourselves by what we do, maybe it's because we can't bear the idea that this beauty and brokenness is not just outside us.

If there's real beauty then there's real value.  If there's real value then there's a real value-giver.  If there's real brokenness then there's real value, destroyed.  If there's real value then there's a real value giver and they will be eager to restore value.

The Christian message is born in the cauldron of beauty and brokenness.  In the beginning, God created and he declared it was very beautiful.  Then, as the story goes, brokenness enters our beauty.  Mistrust into a perfect moment of vulnerability.  Pain shatters perfection leaving a world divided, unequal and hurting.

The good news of the Christian 'gospel' is that God himself has stepped into his beautiful and broken creation.  He is not hiding behind a Facebook profile, a book, a messenger or an institution.  God himself has come face to face with the highest heights of beauty and the deepest depths of brokenness.

The cross where Jesus died shows the brokenness of the world absorbed in one man.  The empty tomb bears witness to the fact that beauty wins.  God wins.

The invitation of Christianity is to allow God to restore you to the person you were meant to be.  As you become restored you will join in the work of restoring beauty in a profoundly broken world.

We believe that you cannot know beauty and brokenness intimately and not be drawn to Jesus – the pinnacle of beauty and brokenness.

**Dan Tyler, Students & Interns Pastor, St George's Church, Leeds.**

# BELIEF

**In a world torn by religious bigotry and division, the Crypt is a sign of hope. Not just hope for those who come through our doors needing help, but a sign of hope for everyone who helps us in our work, whatever their faith may be.**

One of our regular guests, who has known much grief and sadness in her life, is fond of saying "I don't care what religion, race or creed you are: Him Upstairs looks after us all."

Those of us who are employed or who volunteer here know 'Him Upstairs' by many different names.

Our founder was an Anglican priest, whose vision, forged in the furnace of war, went far beyond narrow sectarianism.

Our café is dedicated to St Francis of Assisi: we remember the Franciscan words: 'Preach the gospel wherever you go: use words if necessary.'

So our gospel is Matthew 25:

'I was hungry and you gave me food, I was thirsty and you gave me something to drink, I was a stranger and you welcomed me, I was naked and you gave me clothing, I was sick and you took care of me, I was in prison and you visited me.'

Those of the Jewish community who give so willingly of their time and resources, both financially and through volunteering, may find in 'Sefer Yeshayahu' that the sacrifice that G-d requires is 'to loose the bonds of injustice to share your bread with the hungry, and bring the homeless poor into your house.' Isaiah 58:6,7.

Bagels from the Street Lane Jewish Bakery are particularly popular: especially as a bagel fits in a pocket much easier than a loaf!

For our Muslim brothers and sisters, they find in the Holy Qu'ran many references to charitable giving, as in this translation of Surah 76:8 (Al-Insan): 'And they give food, for the love of Him, to the needy, the orphan, the captive.'

The move-on boxes provided by Leeds Grand Mosque have helped those in need to make a new start, and to settle into new accommodation when they leave us.

Our Sikh friends cook wonderful curries for us every Saturday, thus extending the principle of the 'Langar' - the community kitchen which offers food to anyone who needs it.

For some years now, our guests have benefited from the professional guidance of a Hindu visitor to the

Crypt, who offers practical and knowledgeable advice to those who need to negotiate the complicated benefits and welfare system.

'He gives to all, be they recluses and Brahmins or wretched, needy beggars; he is a giver of food and drink, clothing... lodging and lights.' (Rig Veda 110)

Many of those who support the work of the Crypt would not willingly identify themselves with any religious tradition; yet still they selflessly give of their time and resources, without the hope of any eternal reward.

The Crypt finds a home in the hearts of Christians of many different traditions, who work alongside one another but whom might not attend each other's Churches. Together they serve the Lord Jesus Christ, as they serve plates of food, make beds, clean the rooms, and show a loving and humble spirit to all who come to us in need of help. This, surely, is true worship.

We may thank God that the Crypt provides a place where individual creeds and differences matter less than the desire, given us by God, to love and help

Neville Cohen with the bread Street Lane Bakery donate.

THE STREET LANE BAKERY LS17

Growing Room volunteers take a break from gardening.

'One of the unemployed men who went along to see what was happening at St George's was struck by the fact that Don said he didn't intend to push religion; and that whilst religion was little mentioned, it was evident that the workers and clients at St George's needed this to live.' Find out more about Don Robins on page 10.

Don's very first sermon to St George's Church included this heartfelt plea:

'I appeal to you that there shall be between us all a deep unity, born of the recognition of the Fatherhood of God and the Brotherhood of man. Remember always, God is on the side of the sufferer.'

'In that spirit he began; in that spirit we go on.'

those who are in need. We rely on the prayerful and practical, loving and generous support of all who enable our work together.

In this way, we trust that we are doing the will of Jesus, who prayed that we may all be one.

This ecumenical spirit goes back to the very foundation of the Crypt. Don Robins was the founding secretary of Leeds Council of Churches, at a time when many regarded such an idea as a dreadful heresy.

A volunteer from the Sikh community.

A volunteer from Reach International.

Nurture at Trinity in Leeds.

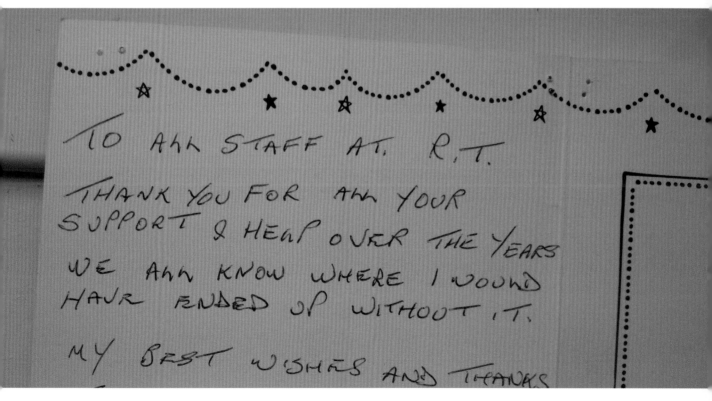

A thank you note from a resident at Regent Terrace.

"Well, I became a Christian in 1995 and that altered my grid references, perspectives and value of life.

I no longer pursued just pure self-interest and money.

I began to see a wider world view, and began to appreciate the value of everyone as an individual.

I wanted to be involved in work that helped people."

**Matthew Nice, Operations Director at St George's Crypt**

# TEAM

## This is a 'day in the life' of our Duty Office who are responsible for managing client referrals.

They sit in a pair of comfy sofas and do the assessment. In 1930 it was 'come in, line up and food was doled out,' and a written record of clients was prepared.

Today we need much more information so we can help clients. We now have a 16-sided form covering recent medical, housing and family history. There's so much information to process.

Putting someone at ease and giving reassurance is all part of the job. It's not another interview for someone to pass... to say the right thing; it's important information to get a full picture so we can help. The staff don't seem fazed by the answers, some of which could make you angry or bring you to tears. It begs the question, 'How does a team cope?'

Is it thick skin? They seem to understand that they are the rock and that they must be strong. If a tear comes, it's important to share it but not break down, to hold fast and reassure the client that they are safe; that everything will be alright.

A bedroom is made up with clean sheets, fresh towels, some toiletries; all checked off ready for the next person. Some Z beds are put out ready just in case they're going to get an extra influx.

The Crypt is open 24/7 and Angels turn up at the most unsociable hour. A wheelchair user has come direct from the hospital.

There is a link project now between the Crypt and the hospitals to stop people just discharging themselves onto the street. The team grows; partnership.

In the old days people would maybe turn up at the door still in their hospital pyjamas.

Now the Crypt ensures a smooth transition and that everything is ready and waiting. All it takes is a phone-call. Other residents offer to help their peers; it's all an extension of the Crypt's organic, dynamic team. Everyone mucks in.

In reception the district care team is signing into the building to see a couple of people. A member of staff leads the way to the clients and finds a quiet space for them to do their work.

The mix of Crypt staff and professionals from other organisations working together is great to watch. The council are here too, talking about available property they have across the city that can accommodate the different needs; an extensive team, dedicated to the work of St George's.

A donation is brought in and directed up to the shop. This opens up another view of the team that operates within the Crypt.

Volunteers from the hostels are working, sorting out the clothes, moving the furniture, helping with the deliveries and you get an idea of how far-reaching, how inclusive the work of the Crypt really is.

It isn't just the paid staff, volunteers, or even the client volunteers that 'make it,' it's about one family beating with one big heart.

Armley feels more than a shop. It's more a part of the community as people come and go and use the café next door. The café is one of three that the Crypt runs across the city.

This gives people who have been through the Crypt some valuable skills in catering and customer service. The menu is comforting and good value. It's real work with real customers, real staff with real stories.

The majority of the café staff have come through the system, even played for the youth side, the under 19's, the under 21's before breaking into the senior team.

The van is filled with some donated food. The van seems to be around Leeds all day long. A couple of clients help with the work. Bread and cakes from a bakers over-order is enough to provide an extra take home for our lunch time opening. As the van is unloaded we see real teamwork in action.

A community fundraiser comes back from a talk at a local school and another is on the phone talking to some volunteers about the bag packing done in a nearby supermarket. Some signs need to be made and collection buckets made ready. Literature is prepared.

Down the corridor is a wind up clock, an original from when they opened in 1930 with a picture of Don Robins next to it. The clock's large numerals provide a steady tick, marking the passing of time down the corridor.

A room is marked 'Meeting in Progress.' The agenda looks like many others, but item one is opening with a prayer.

With all that has changed through the years, would the founding vicar, looking out from his photograph be pleased with what it has become today?

A Hand Up Not A Hand Out

Jo Bedford, Opera North.

**ARMLEY CAFE.**

CHIPS, PEAS
& BRAISING
STEAK
£3.50

**ARMLEY SHOP.**

REGENT TERRACE.

LEEDS MINSTER.

29

# This is Matthew.
# Operations Director at St George's Crypt.

**I oversee the running of the different projects, including the three hostels we have, such as one for men who are still dependent drinkers... that's 10 beds. Another called Faith Lodge which has 15 beds for men who are coming off drink and drugs.**

### What are your reasons for working at the Crypt, what do you get out of it yourself?

Well, I became a Christian in 1995 and that altered my grid references, perspectives and value of life. I no longer pursued just pure self-interest and money.

I began to see a wider world view, and began to appreciate the value of everyone as an individual. I wanted to be involved in work that helped people. Therefore I have spent the last 10 years or so working particularly for third sector organisations.

I happened to get married in 2004, moved to this area and worked in Bradford in a homeless organisation specifically for people on drugs. I saw this job, and it was advertised as a Christian organisation. This fitted in with my values and that's why I came here.

### As a member of staff, do people offload their feelings onto you? Is it hard to deal with?

I think it can be. I met a chap who had been fleeing violence. He was sitting opposite me, and he was talking to me, obviously quite traumatised but there was nothing I could do about his situation, other than listen and try to empathise with him.

On talking to him, he was already housed and therefore couldn't stay here, he actually needed to go back to his accommodation and work with other local agencies on personal safety.

That's what I said to him, and when I told him that, he began to cry. But the tears that he shed, they were tears like a small child, who has just broken their favourite toy. It was recognising that this situation was unfixable there and then.

They weren't tears of 'Oh dear I'm just a bit upset.' They were the tears of a frightened child, not the tears of a grown man sitting opposite me. There was very little I could do.

I wanted to hug him and tell him it would be alright, but it wasn't going to be alright, he was going to have to go back to his current accommodation.

I went back to my office and thought, what do I do about that? In the end it is our job to make sure that they move forward in their lives, working together with all the local agencies to ensure positive steps for everyone.

# PEOPLE

**What would possess a person to work with the smelliest, dirtiest, laziest, most abusive, most drug-addled people in our society? Why would you want to put yourself with the lowest of the low, the worst of the worst?**

Godliness is a faith that supersedes all else. This alone might make you think that helping those worse off than yourself is a path you should take, and worth the sacrifice.

However, faith aside, why would anyone want to go near these modern day lepers?

It's at this point that it is worth addressing a common misconception. Of course people come to the Crypt to 'do good' and in some cases, because of their faith. However, whether we're talking about the staff, volunteers or clients who use our services, other reasons include: teamwork, building skills, developing a sense of family, working for the common good and to work for people... not profits.

In the first instance, St George's Crypt now extends far beyond the original building. It now encompasses the main Crypt, one wet hostel, one dry hostel, three shops, three cafés and an outside catering facility.

The original employees, mainly volunteers from the congregation in the church upstairs, have changed into a professional team of over 50 full-time staff plus part-time and bank staff. Without these, and a good number of regular volunteers, the charity would collapse.

The remit of our charity has also changed. We still keep to our mission statement, meeting the needs of the homeless and vulnerable.

However, St George's Crypt has now organically grown into a broader service, providing support and development from the moment you walk through the front door to the point you move into your own accommodation. All of this requires specialized staffing.

Talent comes in all forms. Be it the receptionist who doubles up as the best support worker money can buy, or support workers who signpost clients to a wide variety of different services.

It could be a chef doubling as a mentor, or training and engagement mentors working hard as project managers, counselling, or in drug and alcohol therapy.

Everyone works above and beyond to provide the best possible service to the homeless, vulnerable and marginalised of Leeds.

Be it those paid by St George's Crypt, or agencies working with us, volunteers, client volunteers; these are the people who make the centre tick, they make all the ligaments move, without seeming to know exactly why.

Are they called? Is it a higher power? Did they go through the same and want to give back? Have they been through the Crypt, seen the good it does, felt it at first hand and decided to make it their life? Is it all of the above and more?

The Crypt is a community, people working together for a common goal. If you ask why people work then you get lots of answers. The overriding fact is that the work is good, that people deserve a second chance, and ultimately that the wider community is failing these people, ostracising them as deadbeats, scroungers, vagabonds, strays. In the Crypt everyone is equal.

The CEO cooks the soup for lunch, everyone eats together, there is always enough to go round even if they have to scrimp and save. There are plans for more; more training, more housing, more catering, all run on the same principles of Christian love not bible-bashing. Lead by example and the rest will follow. And they do follow.

The catering section of the Crypt has 16 members of staff, of which 15 of these have come through the system. 15 of them have worked as client volunteers, been given more responsibility, learnt the trade from the catering manager, walked the line, been given bank shifts and finally full-time employment. No zero hours contracts here!

Within the Crypt itself there are many stories of people working here. Members of staff who used to be clients, individuals who are no longer here, people who have flown the coop and are now living fulfilled lives across Great Britain.

People speak volumes about the life changing work the Crypt does, both to them and through them; so much so that you can't help feeling touched. People really do care. We see it all over our TV screens; apathy to the problems of the world, especially if it

Crypt audience watching an Urban Sprawl performance.

dare encroach on our doorstep, spoil our holiday, or delay our travels.

But the Crypt is a refreshing change, a breath of fresh air and this is in no small part down to the people who give their time on a daily basis.

If you're not used to giving, then this might seem almost sacrificial, but not from our perspective. If you are not used to the cold then the Russian practice of ice swimming will turn your toes, if you're not used to the heat then the desert - well... you get the picture.

What is it that makes those who work at the Crypt have this altruistic nature? Is it something in every one of us? Is it only down to their Christian ideals? Jews, Sikhs, Muslims, Councillors, MP's, all good citizens of Great Britain and beyond already lend their time.

The building itself may be a reconditioned Crypt, and the founder himself one of the greatest Christian Pastors in the UK. A stereotypical view might be that Christianity is steeped throughout the building. There is admittedly a spiritual aura, but you don't feel oppressed.

Take it or leave it, there is no doubt that the aura is good. If you want to walk a journey with Christ then that's good, but no-one's going to string you up if you don't.

And so we find ourselves back at the beginning, with our preconceptions smashed. Who would want to work with the smelliest, dirtiest, laziest, most abusive, most drug-addled people in our society? We do. On walking through the halls of the Crypt you find out a lot about people.

That they have stories. That the staff have stories. That everyone has a story. That they are more than the preconceptions of a bored society looking for a scapegoat.

People are people no matter where we walk. There is little tangible difference between the clients and the staff. There is little tangible difference between the staff of St George's and the staff of the biggest corporations on earth.

Given the opportunity, it does not take that much to turn a life around. Even with the fallen, there is not that much difference between us and them, and the staff at St George's see this.

They nurture this. They close the gap, but also realise that the gap is not that large. In society, we like to think there is a gulf, push it further and further until they become alien.

The good people of the Crypt work hard to draw it tight and therein lies a reason; to bring people together, to be as one, we are all one body and what a terrible shame to try and break it up.

This is John.

One of the things you realise is that everyone is a human being, not 'that alcoholic' or 'that tramp' on the margins of society. Each person has something to give to others, whether they realise it or not. There is something to give for the volunteer as well, part of which is realising your own life is not so chaotic; it gives you a balance on your own life.

I have always known the Crypt was there for people through Brian from Dublin, a drinker from the streets of this city. He introduced me to people from that background, people with a few deep-set difficulties in their lives and I have always tried to support them in some way, not just financially.

In 2013, I was in a group in Woodhouse where we practiced prayer to raise spirituality when Amirah, who was leading the group, said that in her subconscious she saw me at St George's Crypt. This was one of the ways her spirituality worked. Then I got in touch with Tara for volunteering, putting in an application from the internet. Once my references were cleared, I started one month later.

I work mainly Mondays and Fridays with 1 or 2 other volunteers to issue lunch tickets for those who turn up. There is a lunch system in the Crypt where those who are entitled to stay for a period - whether in an individual room or 'in the hub' receive a free meal each day, including the day they leave. If someone is on benefits they are asked to contribute a pound.

There is a high turnover of names, and Tina, who manages the system, updates it throughout the week, which starts afresh each Monday.

St George's Crypt also sell £1 vouchers which can be given to anyone who requires something to eat. I sit at the second reception outside the canteen. If someone is having problems with their benefits or had giros stolen we are the first port of call.

Whilst everyone is asked to produce proof of receiving benefits from the DSS, they cannot always get this.

If suspended from their benefits, which can be for 3 months, we do what we can to ensure people get free meals. The suspension from the benefits system is quite chaotic.

There are a number of people at the moment who came from Eastern Europe to work. If they became unemployed they received an allowance for 3 months, but in 2014 this was stopped due to changes in the law. There is also the occasional pensioner who comes in looking for a decent meal.

Other things that the Crypt supplies is clothing, toiletries, shoes, overcoats, all donated from the public, always useful if you are on the streets.

The Crypt has connections with larger firms who donate goods or services, and even former boxer Amir Khan turned up to serve food alongside members of his charity.

That was quite something, and Amir was gracious enough to spend time with everybody, from the surprised clients to members of the press and everyone who wanted an autograph or a photo got one.

Local restaurants and bakeries donate food. Greggs donate loaves and any unsold, yet edible, goods. The Street Lane Bakery donates bagels, loaves and rolls.

The cooks in the kitchen make something from everything that's donated which can lead to some imaginative meals.

Someone always comes and makes homemade soup, which is delicious, and served alongside a main course and pudding.

Extras, which can vary from donated bread or packets of filled sandwiches, sweets or cartons of milk or flavoured drinks are put into baskets at the back of the canteen so people can help themselves.

I have been volunteering since May of last year and will continue for some time. I used to do graphic design and I am helping on design projects for the Crypt. It takes the work off Andrew's shoulders and gives me the benefit of both seeing something in print and knowing it is aimed at supporting those who are most vulnerable in this 21st century society.

This is Darren.

## What does volunteering give you?

Experience, freedom, knowledge and friends. It might sound a daft idea - but it's also a second home.

I like and enjoy cooking. I can also relate to the Crypt. My dad used to be homeless and I am an ex-alcoholic.

I came to volunteering through a recruitment agency. I had no qualifications and they told me to gain qualifications through volunteering. I have done Food & Safety Level 2. I just need Food & Hygiene and COSHH (Care of Substances hazardous to Health). I do it 3 days a week but I will do more if they need help.

I enjoy responsibility, I am a better worker with more responsibility.

I will continue volunteering until I get a job; I apply for up to 40 a week. When I get a job it will be part time so I can still do voluntary. It's enjoyable; you are more relaxed, comfortable, safe. You feel like you belong here, its very welcoming.

You get to meet different people from different backgrounds, and you see them from where they were, to where they are now.

It's a journey. I would not have known what to expect.

Some people are vulnerable so you don't tend to talk about their situation.

I was with the recruitment agency about 2 months where I did my customer service NVQ. It's making me better prepared with better knowledge of what to do when I do get a job. I definitely want to do catering. Cooking, prepping, serving, cleaning, helping out where help is needed. I also help do events like waiting on and help in the café. You get a certificate in Food & Safety doing this.

I don't like fish! I will cook it but I couldn't eat it. I love making a Quiche Lorraine but I do that at home.

My boss Leanne, she is most easy to get on with. She makes you feel welcome, wanted, that you belong there. She makes you feel like that no matter what you do, and makes you feel comfortable about what you do.

My other boss Dave; he is a very funny sarcastic man; definitely in a nice way.

# ANONYMOUS

**What are your reasons for working at the Crypt?**

The Crypt had a massive impact on me and I really wanted to give something back. I had been homeless for 7 years and a heroin addict and when I came out of prison I ended up at the Crypt. Once I left, I came back to volunteer full-time and after about 8 months I was offered a job and that was over 7 and a half years ago.

**What do you gain from working here?**

Being here at the Crypt is like an extended family, there are no judgements, no people thinking you're a criminal. Here it makes me think, 'that's my past, this is my future.' That's how it was put to me. I had never thought in terms of a future before.

**You say you were homeless for 7 years?**

Yes I was. Before I came to the Crypt I thought that was my going to be my life.

**Did you have any relationship experiences before becoming homeless?**

I hadn't really had relationships before. I didn't really have much of a good family background and it was safer for me to just walk away, but I didn't know anywhere else apart from the streets.

I struggle sometimes because my wife's family is so different to mine and just seeing the way they are with each other was almost alien to me. It just took a while to realise that actually having a loving family is normal, just took me a while to compute that.

**When you came to the Crypt, how did they help you with that transition?**

They just allowed me to be me. That's the best way I can describe it, there was no judgement. What I had done before didn't matter and I was trusted. I remember how amazing it felt to be given a set of keys to the Crypt,.. that level of trust.

I volunteered and they sent me to college for catering and I got my NVQ. No one has ever thought I would achieve anything and they did that for me. When that happens, it makes you want to give back.

**When you were homeless, did you have any opinions on how clothing represented you, or hadn't you really thought about it?**

I suppose in some ways you do, you want to be clean and have clean clothes. But for a lot of people that beg, you have to be dirty in order to make your money.

**They make themselves dirty on purpose?**

Yes, professional beggars do. I was never a professional beggar, but on some days I would make roughly £80-90 quid within 4 hours.

This is why the Crypt have set up a scheme called 'Give me Some Credit.' It's a book of vouchers which the public can buy for a fiver. So if they see someone begging, they can give them a voucher which they bring to us in exchange for a meal and staff can also help them.

When people come here they expect it to be dark and dingy, but it's not like that at all.

It's just about rebuilding these people, there are no judgements.

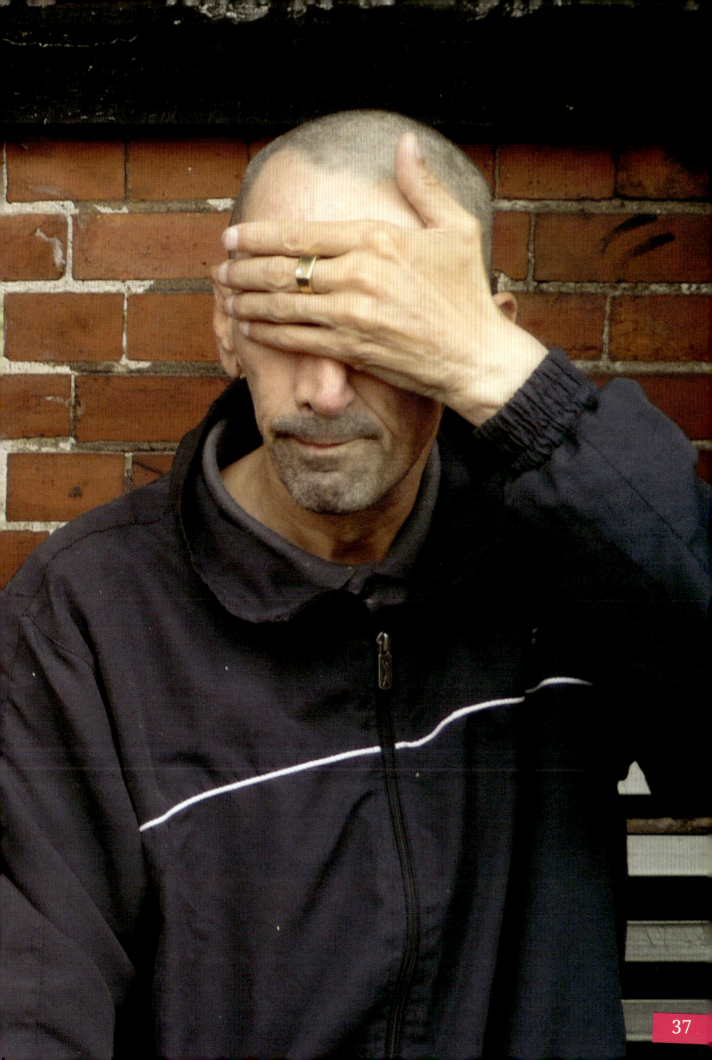

This is Daz.

### Tell me a bit about yourself.

My name is Daz, I've been a client here for 16 years. I did 4 years of voluntary. I was 7 years as a St George's Crypt Warden. I'm 43 and I've spent over 20 years here.

### What was it like being a client here?

Well when I was a client here, they didn't let people in through daylight. It was a family centre through the day. When I was a client back then, if you wanted a bed they didn't have a bedroom, everyone would sleep in the social room.

### What brought you here?

I spent 10 years on the streets in London living like a tramp. I was a mess. I was a tramp. I was originally from Leeds, then I moved to London when I was 16.

I thought there might be something down there, that there wasn't up here.

I mean I couldn't get a job, I had never been to school, no exams behind me, no qualifications so getting a job was just another thing, like living and breathing.

I went to London thinking, it's a higher price of living down there so maybe I would get paid more money and I ended up spending 10 years on the streets.

I woke up next to a lot of people who had passed away at night from choking or the cold. A lot of people were on drugs back then.

### What brought you back to Leeds?

Well because my roots were in Leeds, I was born in Leeds in Armley in 1971. I had a family that I couldn't be bothered with, my uncles and cousins. So I came back to Leeds and I was still homeless when I came back. I didn't look like what I look now; my hair was long and I was pitch black.

So I came back and went to St Anne's Day Centre. A member of staff down there said 'what you need to do is you need to go to the Crypt, get yourself in there for a few nights and get yourself straightened out, cleaned up and put your name down for a council place.'

I came to the Crypt. There was no bedroom, so we were all sleeping on mattresses. I did that for about three or four nights and then I went and put an application down for a council flat. I only applied twice and I got a place in Armley.

Then I met a woman in 2002 and slept with her the first night unfortunately. She fell pregnant and she gave me a beautiful daughter. We fell out three years later and she moved to Cumbria. I've not seen my daughter since.

She left me on the streets so I was back to square one again. I'd done this for 10 years, so I asked myself, 'do I want to keep doing it and end up dead like other people I'd known?'

I didn't want to do that, so I came back to the Crypt. I spoke to one of the team leaders and they got me in a hostel immediately. I had five or six carrier bags of my things on me.

So I was put in the hostel and I was in there for three weeks until I got a place in Bramley. It wasn't really the area that I wanted to be in but it was better than being on the streets.

Going back about twelve or thirteen years when I went to Bramley, when I first got here from London, I had another flat in Bramley. I gave up that flat because of drinking and I couldn't pay the bills and I moved in with another woman in Lincoln Green. We did not have any kids or anything. It was just a relationship and a place to stay.

I came downstairs one morning at nine o'clock and I opened the front door and I got my head smashed in with a baseball bat and I had to have brain surgery. I've got 18 metal pins in me.

I woke up in the hospital after brain surgery and I just thought that everything was going downhill again. A friend came to visit me in the hospital and he got me an emergency place in Bramley.

### Why did someone hit you with a bat?

When I was young I ran away from home a lot, from the age of six living in Morley with my parents.

My dad used to come home every night and just whack, whack, whack me in the face... or my mother when he was drunk. I got sick of it, so I kept running away and this is where my life went downhill.

I used to live in Morley and I went to _____ Lane one night, I was only six years old, and there were caravans everywhere and I fell asleep underneath a caravan. I woke up the next morning and I went into that caravan and I stayed there for six years. And the guy that I stayed with taught me how to fight. He got me through survival.

In 2005-6, I got out again and it must have been bad luck with my third flat as I got another one in Bramley. So I said, 'Well that's it, three times and three times is lucky. Well I've been there ever since.'

### So currently you're working at St George's Crypt?

Yeah, I did four years of voluntary work. I spoke to Chris Fields, CEO of the Crypt and I told him I wanted some sort of voluntary work to take my mind off doing stuff like drugs and drinking. I'd already quit the drinking and the drugs... smoking weed was still a problem in my life but I've overcome that. So he said to me, you can do the door; we need somebody to do the door.

### So what was your role?

I would stand on the door and make sure people wouldn't get in there drunk or come kicking off with the staff.

I was there to back them up. I'm six foot eight, there are not many people in Leeds that are going to want to fight with me. I did that for four years and after those four years Chris called me back to the office and said 'Daz you've done absolutely brilliant, you've changed your life around,' which I had, and he says, 'I want to put you on bank staff,' which is like full-time work but you just didn't have a contract, just when they needed you.

I did it for three and a half years and built up a trust with all the other members of staff and they gave me a full-time contract. I've had that seven years. They gave me the title of St George's Crypt Warden.

My life hasn't been brilliant but I guess you make your life what you want it to be at the end of the day.

When I first came back to Leeds they didn't let people in all day like they do now. Through the daytime they used to have a day service for families to come in, and then at night time six o'clock until nine o'clock they would let everybody in.

### How many people would you get at night?

We're talking one hundred to one hundred and twenty a night. Even now we get one hundred people in everyday. They're not all homeless, maybe twenty people are.

There are a lot of people that come here that have homes. I know half of this lot because I was a client here for sixteen years so I had to shut all them friendships down to do my job, because there are parts of my job that I can't tell other people about because of confidentiality.

It was a bit of a drag because I'd known all these people for a long time, and they had been there for me when I was in trouble.

Now I had pulled through and got a job, and some of them were all right with me, but others were against me now because I was looking at them in a different direction. I mean I had cleaned my life up but they still didn't want to clean their lives up.

### So nobody forced you to clean your life up, you decided it was time?

I got sick to the death of being on the streets and when Jenny went off with my daughter back in 2004. My daughter was four and I haven't seen her since she left, and she's thirteen now.

For the two years that I was living with her, I was doing voluntary work here. She knew I was an ex-client here but I had not told her that I was doing voluntary work because there was a chance of getting a job, and I wanted to surprise her when I got the job so I had something decent to put on my daughters birth certificate. 'St George's Crypt Warden' is much better than 'Homeless alcoholic on drugs.'

You really don't want that on your daughters birth certificate so I told her not to put it on there and then two years later she disappeared. I went back to the street and that's it, I've not seen her since. Now she lives in Cumbria and she's married. I had a great bond with my daughter.

### How have friendships been important in this journey?

I have one client friend who's still a friend. I've known him twenty years. He's stuck by me and I stick by him too.

### What has friendship done for you... from when you left home to arriving at the Crypt?

Well friendships have done nothing for me really. I mean the only friendship I really enjoyed was when I had my daughter. I don't really bother with people. Once I had my full-time job every client that came through the door just shut me out.

They see me around and say 'Hi' to me and tell me I'm looking good so I guess it's something for them to look up to. To see that I've come from down here and now I'm up here. It gives them a bit of a push in the right direction. They can see how much I have changed.

### Do you think it's better to have client volunteers?

We've got a lot of client volunteers here. When I was a client here they never really had client volunteers.

There's a chance maybe that a job might come from that, and because you're a volunteer you get that job and you get off the street.

### How does your job currently work?

I work nine until five, any job in the building I've got it and anything to do with the security of the building.

I am proud of myself now. I've gone through it.

### What advice would you give someone in your previous situation?

If they were in my previous situation I would tell them to quit first because you're going nowhere if you don't

It depends what they're on, I've done every drug on the planet and every known type of alcohol, I think once I even drank pee when I was a tramp in London. I just took a bottle and I drank it and I wasn't even bothered what it was.

Anybody could find himself or herself homeless. In one minute. You could have a nice posh house and be paying your mortgage off, with a nice car and it can all go under just like that.

### What do you think about the council's input in the Crypt?

I think the council's doing a brilliant job at the minute. I think they're in charge of our beds. I think it is a lot better now than what it used to be.

There's a lot of people on the streets that sit there all day and beg but they're not homeless. I know one guy that goes to York every day of the week and he drives there, he's got his own house, and he sits and begs there. A lot of people can sit on the streets and can get sixty quid per day just begging. I could never bring myself to beg.

### Is there something that you hold onto since you left home?

I don't want to remember nothing about my home life or my parents. I try to forget it. It's like when I got my head smashed in, I've been trying to forget about it since then but every single night I go to sleep and I dream about it. I could tell you the entire story about how I woke up with a pool of blood around my head and a chunk of skull sat there in the blood. I could get my fist in there.

When I woke up and I came round, my eyes were all blurry. The only thing I could see were two green objects standing next to me, which later turned out to be ambulance workers. I got in the back of the ambulance with my own two feet. I literally walked into the ambulance and I sat down, they shut the ambulance doors and on the inside of the window I could get a perfect reflection because its blacked off from the outside.

I could see my own brain and I can't go to sleep and forget it. It's all there and it's part of my life. The only thing that ever stopped me from dreaming was smoking weed, but I don't ever want to go down that lane again.

Daz

The donations we receive are vital for the Crypt.

"The reason I became a councillor was to give people a voice who do not have a voice."

I became a City Councillor in 2010, the first Leeds City Councillor for the homeless. I have always known St George's Crypt and homelessness as I had experienced it as a young man. I had been homeless for 3 months in Scunthorpe, having lost my job and had all my clothes stolen.

In 2012/13, I became a lead member for homelessness with responsibility for working with organisations supporting the homeless. My role as a city councillor was to help the relationship improve between St George's Crypt, the council and other organisations helping homeless people.

You have to take it seriously; especially in freezing temperatures, you see the homeless out there and I was linking the homeless to St George's Crypt.

I would go out in my car to ensure they were not out on the street.

In conjunction with St George's Crypt we employed an organisation to do city sweeps; going out at different times to come across homeless people on the streets to help people.

There is a severe weather protocol; where below certain temperatures extra beds are made available. I do not want anyone to freeze on the street. I have seen what the homeless experience.

I saw; lets call him 'Frank' in the arches. He said to me he would die. I tried to help, and tried to get him to St George's. However, a few days before, someone had given him £20 when he was begging. He spent it all on ale and went into hospital.

After he came out, I saw him on the Friday, but he was again too drunk to be helped. He told me he knew he was going to die. I made a commitment with him then that I would attend his funeral. Given that experience, I was determined that no person was going to have to sleep on the streets, so I tried to make things run smoothly for people.

The prison gap; I visited the prison to talk with people because at church one Sunday. Two people came to me asking for money as they were just out of prison. I asked why they had nowhere to go. The reason was they had given a false address so that they could be released from prison.

I would not give them money but I re-doubled my efforts with St George's. I was part of the start of the voucher scheme so that no one would be hungry or needed cash. Nobody was given money for alcohol, but were able to get food so they wouldn't die.

So for those out of prison, and who could not get somewhere straight away, they could get food on most days of the week.

The scheme involves books of £5 vouchers that can be bought from the libraries or shops, such as in Horsforth, Wetherby and Beeston.

So instead of giving money, you can give a beggar a voucher for a meal. The hungry would have food and those who were not hungry would refuse the voucher.

It's a dilemma; what you could do and what you should do. Giving money to beggars can kill them. I am referring back to Frank's situation again.

Now I volunteer for St George's Crypt on Mondays by driving a van, and collecting stuff from supermarkets and businesses such as fruit and veg shops. I collect the goods and bring it back to the Crypt to feed people.

Through the partnership between Leeds City Council and St George's Crypt, you can quantify the numbers that have been assisted, but you cannot quantify the effect on people in terms of physical, mental and self-worth that this partnership achieves.

# JOURNEYS

## Where does homelessness start and stop?

Homelessness is a dirty word. Often associated with the lowest of the low, the scroungers, the beggars, the untouchables – those we would not like to see and will never be like. 'How far away from ourselves that image is,' we think and yet how little do we know.

The historic image of the homeless, a gnarled, weather worn individual, normally a man, normally in drink, could not be further from the truth.

These are people, these are our brothers and sisters. As Jesus himself said, 'our mothers and fathers and we bear some responsibility to understand' that their story is not one of avarice, of laziness or an unwillingness to get a job, to integrate with a society they avoid.

Homelessness has many faces, and those faces are constantly changing. From the young lad leaving home and not being able to find any fortune in the great wide world, to the man who lost his job, lost his family, lost his home and having nowhere to go... who ends up on the street. The dirt conceals a much more human tune; a tune we as a society are unwilling to listen to. When the discord hits we see the superficial and rarely look any deeper.

Even if we did, we would soon stop because the stories hit so close to the bone that they themselves are fearsome.

It is not nice to hear of the girl prostituted from the age of 4, or the man whose family deserted him because he could not keep them in the lifestyle they were used to, or the ground-breaking researcher who had a nervous breakdown and was promptly dumped by his entire social network.

It draws a mirror to the face that we do not like to see, the guilt of passing someone on the street and knowing that it could be me dilutes into 'it's just another homeless bum.'

It becomes easy to give the money, to assuage the guilt, to pay for the drink and drugs or at least tell ourselves blithely that this is what they will probably do. After all, that caused problem didn't it? Isn't it of their own making and solution?

But the problem is deeper. The journey does not begin with drink, drugs or a wish to live free with no responsibilities. The five main causes of homelessness are domestic violence, eviction, relationship breakdown, lack of accommodation and financial breakdown as a result of joblessness.

Mix two or three of those together, or add in underlying mental or physical health issues and there is a recipe for disaster. We may think 'It couldn't happen to me,' but it so easily could.

There is a saying here at St George's Crypt that it takes one month from losing your job before you might find yourself homeless; mortgage repayments, rent arrears, car, TV or energy bill creditors on the doorstep and the journey begins. And where do you go?

Have you ever thought that homelessness may breathe down your neck? How many people know how to navigate the homelessness system, and yet how easy it is to fall into the murky waters.

'It wouldn't happen to me – I've got friends.'

But how long will that line of credit extend? How many sofas can you sleep on before all bridges are burnt? How many meals will be provided before people expect something in return... there's never a free lunch is there?

And then, wandering the street, dissolute, lost and in need you hear of a light shining in the darkness, a beacon of hope and the journey moves on.

From its roots as the Crypt of St George's Church, St George's Crypt has come a long way from its inception 85 years ago. When Don Robins set the charity up, little did he know that the mainly volunteer led organisation would become a much bigger organisation with two hostels, three cafés, three shops and be one of the best known and most loved charities serving the city of Leeds.

Instead of sleeping on pews, there are now rooms and beds. Instead of a small tea service with soup and sandwiches staffed by volunteers from the Church, there is now a fully-fledged catering social enterprise employing 13 staff, of which 96% are ex-service users.

This social enterprise not only cooks the three meals provided daily to the most marginalised and vulnerable of Leeds, but also staffs the cafés, providing catering across the city and beyond, giving a step-up and the possibility of training and employment to the same marginalised and vulnerable people who would not find support anywhere else.

Spurred on by the grace that imbues every corner of the charity, St George's Crypt fulfils its original mission statement to serve the needs of the most marginalised and vulnerable, those that no-one else will.

Residents of Faith Lodge.

Our clients come to us from all backgrounds. Possibly jobless, potentially with historic abuse, broken families, and may even have turned to drink or drugs to alleviate a pain that society will not accept knocks on the clean clear glass door of the Crypt.

He or she will walk into a warm reception staffed by people who refreshingly do not see love as a barrier, as a health and safety risk, or as a safeguarding nightmare.

As the Crypt has expanded, so have the services it offers. Housing support, training and engagement, mental health services, physiotherapy, drug and alcohol counselling, opera, drama and art to name a few. All of these are there to steady the ship, build confidence, developing people that have been thrown on the scrap-heap by a society that has forgotten compassion, or at least decided that it is much too hard.

Manners cost nothing, but we seem to think that some are not worthy of these emotional responses.

Calm. Many of those who have been residents of the Crypt have described it as the 'eye of a storm,' a sea of tranquillity in a turbulent ocean. When their bearings have been off, St George's has stepped in, steadied the rudder and put them on course for smoother sailing.

The Crypt has evolved; more than a soup kitchen, more than a shelter, more than a roof. It tries to provide a way forward; to link people up with housing, link them up with the council, support through the endless forms and phone calls and meetings and set them up for the next stage on their journey.

85 years ago did Don Robins sit down and think that the Crypt he dug out would still be providing support, structure, and care to some of the most vulnerable and marginalised people in Leeds?

Did he think that the need would have expanded the Crypt into a fully-fledged, multi-disciplined training centre with great outcomes?

Did he think that the rich stories permeating the very fabric of the building would continue, turning the building into a physical manifestation of the journeys it has helped in?

This is the rich tapestry St George's Crypt has sewn into the psyche of Leeds  This unconditional approach helps all that enter its doors, with an ability to build up those broken and put them on the road to recovery. It's a very Christian love without the sermonising.

It should remind us all that whilst this is God's country, there is still an awful lot to be done, a long road to walk and we need to walk it together. All of us need to engage on the journey to confront the issues around homelessness.

We are all fallible and we all make mistakes. We are all human and it is this, not the misrepresented stereotype, that we need to follow.

Give people some credit.

As they say on the game-shows 'it could be you!'

# JOURNEYS

This is Lee.

Volunteering 7 – 8 months.

I recently got out of prison in November 2013. I was fed up sitting on my bum all day. It gives motivation, gets me out, when I apply for a job it looks good that I have been volunteering.

It is better than being in the big house. I have done quite a tour of the jails:

2004 Doncaster, Marshgate, Northallerton, Deerbolt

2007 Armley, Everthorpe

2012 Armley, Wealstun, Pentonville

I get on well with the other volunteers; like a big family really when we are all together. I work in the kitchen, help prepare buffets, get them sent out, clearing, washing up and work at the Trinity and the café in Armley.

It is welcoming. We do get on well, not one member of staff has had an argument, you can ask for a bit of help or a bit of food to take home; they give a helping hand; they never/rarely say no. It has given me a bit of self-confidence to get into the role of working again, to get into the routine of work.

I am not at home arguing with the missus because we are under each other's feet. We are doing different things, so we argue less. It gives her a bit of space and me a bit of a break.

I have been in prison a couple of times but I am a bit older now. It is keeping me out of trouble, out of the way of the police. I had never done volunteering before. I was hot-headed and I do not want to go back so I am doing things differently.

It's giving knowledge; keeping me out of trouble. So I can carry on with my probation; the licence ends in July - that's not far away now.

I have done it, I really do not want to go back. I want a quiet life, settle down, a stress free life. I am nearly 30 now. I don't want to show my babies that I am in and out of jail. It is just an existence, you get given a number. I know all my numbers I have had.

Lee has now left the Crypt and has a full-time job.

This is David.

What were your reasons for coming here?

Sour relationship and bad past.

Is your relationship the reasoning for being here?

She was a drinker and I was a smoker.

Did you rely on each other?

Things went pear-shaped when she started stealing my money, so I had to get out of that relationship and got myself into another relationship which was even worse.

Where are you from originally?

Newcastle.

I definitely thought you sounded Welsh.

Laughs. I have a Yorkshire accent, I have a Geordie accent, I have a Welsh accent.

Are you happier now that you have been coming here?

They took me off the streets before the cycling for Tour de France. They gave me the opportunity to either go to prison or come here. I chose to not go to prison.

What did they say they were going to take you to prison for?

Just for being homeless, just lock you up like that.

That's awful.

It is ridiculous isn't it?

What is your employment background?

I'm a chef, for pies and puddings. I'm a Pastry Chef.

Great. Did you have your own business or work for someone?

No no, I started off in Newcastle College, the only way I could get in was hairdressing, you could put your name down for just about anything, mechanics, brick laying.. and then applied for a food course.

What's the best thing about baking?

Eating it.

I would say that too.

Nah people saying it is nice, I really appreciate that.

Would you like to get back into it?

I would like to be closer to town from where I am, because I'm in Beeston at the minute. It is a 45 minute walk and back, so I bought myself a scooter last week

I used to have one of those. Important question. Do you bake wedding cakes?

Laughs. Not my speciality.

Do you feel like it has been a challenge to get a job because of your past?

It is hard because my past has a way of fighting back. When I become really settled, when I thought this is it. I fell in love, and they say there is an Adam and Eve for everybody in the world, they put me in Newcastle and her in Finland. I met her in a park, and my heart pumped.

So she is in Finland now?

My mam said it is always best to get your past out, I have 3 kids, we were going to get married and 3 days before the wedding she was with my best mate. I paid for the church, flowers.. everything. Everything came out my back pocket, everything.

How old are your kids now?

Oh um, eldest daughter is 21... just had a baby boy, so I'm a Granddad. A 17 year old son and a 16 year old daughter.

This is Tony.

**Where are you from, and how long have you been coming to the Crypt?**

Hartlepool originally, and 5 years.

**What were your reasons for coming here originally?**

I came to Leeds, from a relationship breakdown in Middlesborough. I had a serious mental breakdown, health issues, no where to live and everything else.

Nowhere to go. The street wardens picked me up and took me up to the Crypt. I got given food, shelter, clothing. Saved my life, what more can I say.

**So this has been a huge turnaround for you?**

Yeah massively.

**Did you have any friends or family when you were in that situation on the streets?**

No no, I've been on my own since I was 15. I lost all my family when I was 15. My mum, my dad and my two sisters just gone in one day.

**Was that an accident?**

House fire. I was at school, they were trapped and couldn't get out. That was about 25 years ago now.

**So, you were at school?**

Yeah I was at school, came home and there's your wrecked house and no parents.

**Did you finish school?**

I didn't. I couldn't physically.

**Has this effected you job wise, what have you been doing?**

I have mainly been training and volunteering, because there is no point in me applying for a job, because I've got drugs in my previous, got criminal record, and employers aren't gonna wanna know.

**And it's bad that they don't understand the person you are first isn't it?**

They see the criminal record straight away and think, uh scumbag!

They don't see me for me, or see the reasons behind what I did what I did. That's the thing.

I've been here 5 years and got a chemical qualification, a gardening qualification and that's all from here.

It puts me in good stead for when I go for a job. Because here they can say 'he's done that for us.'

**So you feel this has skilled you up for the next stages of your life?**

The next 10 or 20 years of my life are sorted because of here. If it wasn't for here, where would I be?

**Are you volunteering here to help other people also? What do you gain?**

A sense of well being and satisfaction, because these things helped me. And if I weren't helping them, what would I be doing? I would be sat around doing nothing.

I come in, give my time, and it makes me feel better in myself, knowing that I have given something back to people that have helped me and saved my life.

Even when one person at the end of the week comes up to you and says thank you for what you did, it makes you feel worthwhile. I come from nothing, I've had nothing, and I've just helped you.

**Is it nice to know you are building skills?**

Yeah it is. I can get lots of references and qualifications from here. Training from OCN. I've been given a certificate from Chelsea Flower show, and I am the man responsible for this garden right here.

I did all this a couple of years ago. Basically I've got all my certificates from here.

This is Jonathan.

How long have you been coming to the Crypt?

Quite a while now.

What do you like about it?

The staff. They are friendly and they help you. They help you get back on your feet and that.

What were your reasons for coming here?

I did have my own place and that, I let my mates move in, and they would smoke, do drugs and what have you. I had to go see the landlord and they told me they were going to kick me out, I came to the Crypt because I don't get on with my sisters.

I feel this has been more my home due to the violence I went through as a kid. I am a lot more happier here.

What are your hopes afterwards?

Hoping to get my own place and that, the staff at Regents Terrace will help me find somewhere to live.

Jonathan moved to Regents Terrace in August 2015. This is his next step forward in recovery. He is currently volunteering at the Crypt and trying to reduce his alcohol intake. We wish him all the best!

"We ring the bell as a call to prayer."

This is Darren.

Where are you from?

Dewsbury.

How long have you been coming to the Crypt?

5 years.

What were your reasons for coming here?

I had a nervous breakdown due to depression, I couldn't cope and it was the only place I could turn to. You feel safe here.

Did you have any family of friends you could turn to?

I just learned to do stuff myself.

Because I'm a fashion student, do you think fashion has changed the way people think of you, or do you not really have an opinion?

Fashion has changed a lot to how it was years ago.

Do you just think as long as you have clean clothes you're fine?

Yes.

What is your educational background?

I passed Art at school, Science and Geography. But because I am slightly dyslexic I wasn't put in for Maths, so I can't do Maths or tell the time.

I didn't pass Maths at school either

I love reading though.

This is Scott.

**How did you find the Crypt? How did you come to be here?**

I came to live back in Leeds from where I used to live in a hostel in Bradford. I came back to be in Leeds to live in a hostel along Whitehall Road. When I first moved back here, basically all I had was the clothes I was stood up in.

So I was asking, 'is there anywhere while I get my benefits sorted out,' 'is there anywhere I could get some food without actually going into Tesco's or somewhere and stealing it.' And a couple of the residents were on their way to the Crypt so they actually brought me here. And that was 15 years ago.

**Wow. So how did you get to be in the situation that meant you were just in the clothes you were stood up in?**

Well, when I used to live with my parents I used to go out on the beer all the time. And it just got to the stage of me drinking, just started getting worse and worse and worse. I ended up losing job after job 'cause I'd either turn up half drunk or just didn't turn up at all. It just got to the stage where my dad gave me the ultimatum, 'curb your drinking or basically pack your bags and do one.'

When you're like 21/22 you think 'yeah I know what I'm doing and I'm king of the world,' so I chose to pack my bags and go. It wasn't until a month into it all I was like 'yeah, really picked the wrong path.'

**Yeah. So, how are you finding it at the Crypt?**

Well, I've been volunteering here for about 8 and half years, that's how I'm here now. It's changed a hell of a lot compared to what it was like 15 years ago when I first come. I'm being brutally honest, back then it used to be rough!

I mean there used to be fights every night, there'd be chairs going up in the air. It's more like a 'Daddy Daycare Centre' now compared to then. Don't get me wrong, it's all obviously changed for the better but like I said back then it was proper rough.

**So what sort of things do you volunteer with?**

Usually in the kitchen, doing the catering side. If I'm not needed in there I'll go out with Ian, the van driver, doing deliveries and pick-ups. To be perfectly honest, I'm a jack-of-all-trades. They're usually the two main things. I've done the door and make sure people who are actually on restriction can't come in.

**Is there anything else you'd like to add?**

Nothing I can think of, no.

**Think you've covered it all. Thank you very much.**

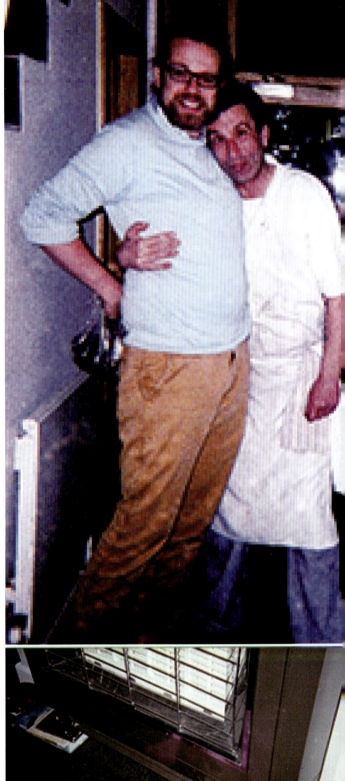

All of these images were taken on film by clients of the Crypt.

This is Bev.

**The day that brought me here I was in such a mess. I got up at six o'clock in the morning and I threw a few things in a bag and decided that I was getting on a train and getting out of the area and the situation that I was in.**

I was taking a leap of faith that what would be on the other side was better than what was here for me. I felt if I stayed there, then I wouldn't have been alive towards the end of the year.

I remember I was absolutely terrified, my heart was pounding. Getting out the house without getting caught, waiting for the train at the train station and getting on the train. But I hadn't thought any further than that.

And when I got here, I went to housing, and I was directed here to the Crypt and that's where things started turning around. So the leap of faith was right. Just do it, just get out of here, just get on the train and do it.

### How old were you?

Well this Thursday is my three year anniversary of being here at the Crypt. I think I was about forty two.

It was weird, I don't know.

I feel like while I was here I was just this little shadow, just this very very tiny person. And I remember people talking to me and asking me things like, 'are you alright?' or 'do you want to come here.' I can always remember one voice, a name but not a face, and it was Kim asking me if I wanted to come to the theatre, 'would you like to do this,' and I didn't want to.

It's taken me a long time and a haul to get to where I am now. There's so many changes. I look back and I think, 'when did that happen?' When did I stop being like that and when did I start feeling great?

One of my quotes and the best way I can describe what happened before was; 'certain very few bright and happy moments' (I used to call them Kodak moments). That's over forty years, but now its like the last few years have gone that quick and everything is bright and colourful and the Kodak moment has become like one long video.

So if I ever have a down moment, it's like it's there and then its gone again and everything's really good.

I said to one of my colleagues last week, that sometimes I can stand there and be out in the garden or look out the window, and even if it's a horrible weather day I can just look out and think; is this real?

It's like when I had my operation, did I slip into a coma and am I in an asylum and I've gone into my own mind? Because if it is, I don't want to wake up because sometimes I just can't believe it.

### Tell me a bit about your role at the moment?

My main job is the housekeeping, cleaning and the client rooms. Trying to get a bit of extra cleaning done. I think the main thing is just to keep my strength and keep being me.

Because, to quote somebody, "We build you from the inside," so the most important thing here is to keep growing and keep building myself up.

As many times as I slide down or fall, I'm always helped back up again and I get up a bit stronger each time.

### So the Crypt is helping you build your strength?

Yeah, my sense of me, which is something I never had before.

### If you can describe yourself in one word what would it be?

Finally me. I said to Andrew last week that when I was a kid I used to imagine that one day the space ship was going to come and take me back home, because I didn't feel like I belonged.

### What have you achieved since you arrived at the Crypt?

I've re-sat my English from entry level up to the equivalent of O-level. I've got all three certificates; entry level, level one and level two. I have the equivalent of O-Level in English.

I've got a mental health awareness certificate from Bradford distance learning. I've got NVQ level two in cleaning and support services. To narrow it down, level two pass is bio clean up, the prevention and control of infections.

The first year I was here I got a flat, and it was in the wrong kind of environment. But I had to have an operation, and it was the first time I had been in the hospital and I was terrified. I had to have a long time away from here while recovering for the operation.

So my mind-set went down again and over that Christmas I had quite a big breakdown again, and I didn't want to talk to anybody.

But then I came down on that January and I completely broke down, and since then it's just been rebuilding myself again. I think that day of my complete crumble is what I needed to finally start building myself up again.

It's like the suicidal thoughts aren't here anymore, so things started building up from there and I started back volunteering. It was during then that I came back from that January to the next Christmas that I got most of my studies done. I did my Maths and English.

### So the year went really quickly.

I've volunteered, and I've done a traineeship. I came back volunteering again and now I'm on staff, but it does feel weird being on the staff because I look at the staff and I've always looked up to them because they're like management and they're in the office doing such a hard job, and then there's just little me.

From the minute I came in, they've all been my support. So it's kind of weird being on the same level.

### So your job helps you build up your inner strength?

Yes, because I used to be really, really bad with social anxiety. Even to the point where if I was stood here and round the corner was a lot of people, I would shake and I couldn't breathe.

I had really bad panic attacks. I don't know when that stopped. I only noticed it last year while I was having a conversation with somebody who suffered from it. I still get a bit anxious now and again, but not to the full panic attack, can't breathe stage that I used to.

And here I see many people have come through what I have, and I'm not alone. Some of the things that I have gone through with my mental health, a lot of people have gone through that here. Maybe not the same circumstances that have developed, it but it is great to know that you're not alone.

It's like a little bubble of craziness sometimes, where you can be a little bit crazy because it is okay to be you and that's all that is has to be. Just be you, heal yourself and be you.

Don't be what somebody out there wants you to be or expects you to be. It's helping you become who you are meant to be and I still don't know who that is. I'm not at the end of the journey, it is still going.

### Do you have any plans for the future? Within the next two years what's your plan?

No, because two years from now I'll be like 'oh, how did I get here'. Last time I was asked this question was when I came back in that January and it was Lent.

I was being interviewed for Radio 5 Live and I got asked the question, 'Where do you see yourself in five years?' I don't know. I'm just not thinking about it. I'll see what happens when I get there. I'll wake up one day and realise I'm 120, how did I get here?

### How do you feel as a woman in the Crypt? Because there is quite an unbalanced ratio of men to women in the Crypt.

I've never really taken it into consideration really. I've always just been one of the gang. I get on with the lads. I think when I was a resident here it was only me and all the lads but I never felt uncomfortable. I always felt safer around the lads, I don't know why but I always got on and I give them cheek as much as they give me because I know where I stand with them. Men are easy to read actually.

### Can you tell me a bit about your friendships in the Crypt

It's like a big happy crazy family here. We're all feeling a loss coming up because we've got three interns here. One we've been working closely with, and it's going to be a shame, but things move on.

We get some brilliant characters coming through here. They just brighten my day up.

### Tell me one situation that has brightened your day.

The leggings. Somebody got a little bit mixed up. They were like underwear leggings, and they thought they were like 'wear about outside leggings' and she shouted at me "do you like my new leggings!" and I was like 'Oh you need to go and put some pants on!!!'

Little things like that, you may not realise at the time, make your day.

Today, somebody actually remembered me as soon as I came in. They called me by name, which was really good. I told him that as well, that he really made me smile.

Sometimes we should keep an emotional distance, but sometimes the client just gets to you. But the good that I see done here every day, I mean I am not the first person or the last person that will turn around and say that 'if it were not for the Crypt I don't know where I'd be.'

There's so many people over the years that have said that, and so many will continue to say it. They're not interested in how much money you have in the bank, or the fact that you're vulnerable or you're easy pickings and we can manipulate you, or we can do this and that.

All they're interested in, is picking you up and helping you heal.

I've never known anything like here, it is amazing here and it is great to be a part of it.

If God gives his toughest battles to his strongest soldiers, then he's got a very strong crew with the staff that work here in the Crypt. I couldn't do their job.

That why I like doing the cleaning. Sometimes they have to tell me to go home.

Some of the clients know that I've been here as a resident and some don't. Some of them have seen my story and then they look at me now. I see that I can be some kind of inspiration to them. Just don't give up.

We never give up. Three years on, I'm still vulnerable, I don't think there will ever be a time when I'm not. There are certain things you just have to accept that are a part of you now.

### Are you religious?

I never used to be. I remember once I was leaving a friends house and I was walking. It was a summer night around ten o'clock and I used to walk past this church and it was the weirdest experience. It's like I walked through a void, there was no sound from here to there, and then suddenly there was a gush of wind and you could hear the traffic again.

It was like that day I got on the train. Strong as anything, a leap of faith. So yeah, I do believe.

I don't know what it was. I'd never experienced anything like it. It's not really about religion but more about faith.

# People don't see who

# **you** used to be

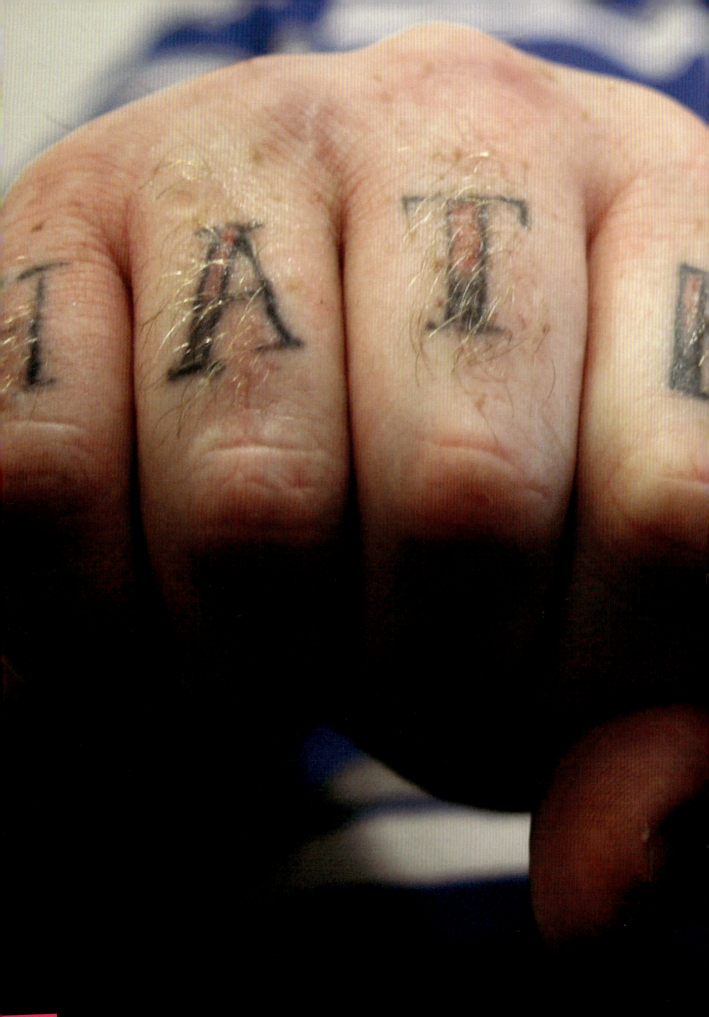

You should never judge a person until you have lived that persons life experience.

**How do you see yourself? When you wake up in the morning and look in the mirror what do you see? Do you even look in the mirror before following a routine? Shower or bath? Special soap, teeth cleaned, nails scrubbed and then the naked body is ready to be clothed.**

How many laundry products are there these days? Hundreds? Thousands? Nowadays a shirt is just for a day, then straight in the basket. Trousers and jumpers might make two, maybe three days at a push but the smallest stain and they follow the same route.

Exercise has taken centre stage and they need a separate wash, maybe a separate product. Husbands, wives, children, grandchildren; they all need dermatological this or specially fragranced that.

And so the body is clean, the hair washed and conditioned, the shirt and trousers ironed, everything smelling fresh and clean, some people skip breakfast some people won't and then outside.

A car? Walking? Cycling? Each has an image, a particular style. What kind of a car? Is the walk good exercise? Does the cyclist have the best suspension, the latest gear, a cool helmet? So even before we get on the road to work we have to tip-toe a minefield.

Perception came to Adam, and now we cannot stand in front of our best friends without our armour. We have created these needs, and now we are slaves to them.

So imagine there is no mirror. There is no way to check how you look. There is no shower. There is no soap. You have no idea how you look when you wake up, how your breath smells but you can guess.

We've all licked our arms and breathed on them. We've all sniffed our pits. If we don't someone else will.

Some clever-clogs will make a face, reel away, ask what you ate last night or if you brushed your teeth, had a shower this morning. And if you dared not spray. We all know the feeling of not smelling nice. Perversely it makes you sweat all the more.

You dig into a black bin bag. No cupboards. The place where people normally put their rubbish is the place you pull your week old, month old, who knows how long ago it was since these clothes were washed and pull them on. Are they wet? Jogging home through the mud and the rain opening the door and the heating is on.

Everything straight into the machine and sparkly clean. Is it cold? No thermostat to put in advance or boost. No settee to settle into, wood-burning stoves all the rage and the 44 inch flat-screen to lull you to bed. No warm blanket to pull over then to bed.

Just living in that skin will have a shattering effect on confidence. Just walking around with one or two of those conditions in place.

It's not that the shower, soap, clean clothes or car is not working. An excuse can simply be found for each of these. The lack of all of them is the foundation, and being in a worse state starts to become the norm.

Perception hits the most marginalised the hardest. Those that are furthest away from the social norm are the most noticeable. Multimillionaires are very perceptible but also able to disguise themselves behind their money; the homeless cannot.

The homeless must trudge from place to place, no place to call their own, all their possessions in one bag; not Vuitton or Prada but normally a black bin liner. As people take a wide berth, cover their noses if they get too close, whispering insults and emanating fear, these rejected souls disappear.

But it's all their fault, isn't it? They take the drugs, they don't want to work, they scrounge off the system. It's their fault that education failed them, the system fails them, they were abused, their family breaks down, they lose their job.

They want the vagabond lifestyle, the world of drink, that free and easy life. They made their bed, so now they must sleep in it.

But no one wants to be different, to be marginalised, to be ostracised without a care for the underlying issues.

The hard facts are that we shy away; it's much easier to blame them, to look down on them, to make it all their fault and believe the wide reaching stereotypes of scroungers, deadbeats. To pity them, to throw them a few pence to allay our guilt and to walk on by.

Under this immense social strain, without any thought of what is happening, what has happened inside the lives of these humans, these people, our individual walks through the doors of St George's Crypt.

Perception tells him or her that they will be given short shrift; it happens everywhere else after all.

Just the material perception of the homeless is enough to depress, and this doesn't take into account any personal issues, the obvious financial issues, social, mental health or physical problems that are faced through a life on the streets.

We have our own internal perception, confidence or lack thereof which is exacerbated or abated by the view the world has of us. Rock stars may have really bad personal hygiene but the world forgives them.

Footballers may have strong opinions but their fans still idolise them. Models may promote unhealthy body complexes but we still love them.

Our individual may stink and not be forgiven, be loud and obnoxious and not idolised and stick thin but unloved. Pushed to the margins by society, pushed to the margins with a symphony of issues, all the dissonance resonates the pain.

And so there is the expectation, there is the perception; another agency that will throw me out, that will speak with forked tongues, that will say yes on the one hand whilst opening the door and lining up the boot on the other.

Frustration and anger at never being included, never being equal, never being loved, just another unwanted statistic that can't hold down a tenancy, that can't hold down a job, that can't get a shower and be normal. And what is this normal?

If normal is Aphrodite, then we are all ugly. If normal is sterile, then we are all unclean. If normal is Samson, then we are all weak.

At St George's Crypt, we try and rework these perceptions. There are numerous programmes, engagement activities, training opportunities for clients to choose from. You don't have to be staying at the Crypt to engage, their sessions are open to anyone and everyone.

This is one of the many steps that the Crypt employs to break internal perception and boost confidence whilst giving the external a makeover.

From the first step through the door you can start, and are actively encouraged to turn your life around.

Showers are offered plus a change of clothes and all toiletries. If you are staying in one of the rooms, then you get a welcome pack that includes a fresh towel, toothbrush, toothpaste and soap for any immediate physical needs.

3 meals a day prepared by trained chefs and volunteers, some of whom have come from the same place. Volunteers who know how easy it is to become homeless, to lose everything, and who are trying to redress the balance. People who have been given a chance to prove themselves.

People. Having this peer network in place, people who have experienced the same looks, the same disregard and the same loneliness. To see them succeeding and engaging breaks down the barriers that an apathetic society puts in place.

People start to open up. If allowed, we quickly realise that it isn't a choice, it's not what anyone would want and the stories are more heartbreaking, more intense than anyone should have to bear.

These histories, weighed down by the exclusion, the disinterest, the ignorance of the wider world serves as a prison to the soul.

How can people move on, develop and heal if not freed from such a mantle? Walking around as a number, another horrible story that no one wants to cope with and why not incubate yourself against such oppression? Without love, what kind of armour must we wear to protect ourselves from a never-ending onslaught?

Perception can change, not only that of the outside world but more importantly the way we feel inside, the way we meet life, take on the strains and stresses of, at times, a foreboding world.

The work that St George's Crypt engages in, taking people at their lowest, when they are most broken, and helping them fix themselves, never giving up, walking a slow and often arduous journey with them can at times seem thankless.

But it is the small miracles, the people coming out of their shells, the harsh realities, the smiles and laughter, the acceptance and development in so many tangible and intangible ways that make St George's Crypt a bastion of hope for those most in need.

Leave the military and you face losing your identity.

Illustrated by Joe Hawkins, a Student at Leeds College of Art.

Russ had to leave the Marines after 8 years of service because of a motorbike injury.

He said that this was like leaving his family, and he struggled without the camaraderie. After being taught how to drink during his service, this is what he turned to when he left.

He also developed PST because of an experience whilst in the service.

This came back to him when his dad died after leaving the Navy.

He then turned to drink, lost his family, then his job, then his house, until he ended up on a street drinking, with nowhere to go.

Illustrated by Joe Hawkins, a Student at Leeds College of Art.

When you're in a shop archway with rats running over your feet, you don't care about other things.

Material stuff means nothing, who gives a damn, you can just get another one.

After leaving the army, Addy left to live with his girlfriend, but couldn't be with her any longer and moved to Leeds to live with his Mum.

With no job and a lot of old friends pressuring him into going out... he drank a lot, until it came to the point where he moved out because he was too embarrassed for his Mum to see him in that state.

So he ended up on the streets.

Stealing beer from shops because he had nothing to lose anymore.

Being a solider meant nothing.

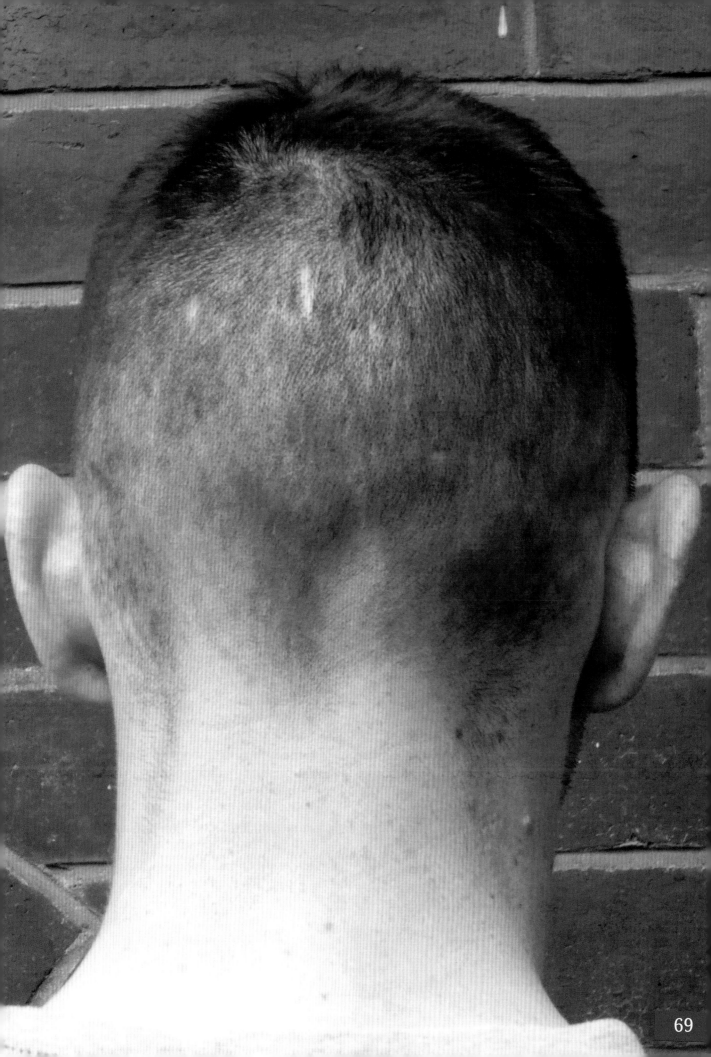

# PARTNERSHIPS

Birds of a feather stick together or opposites attract.  Both could be used to describe the amazing working, voluntary and financial partnerships the Crypt has developed over the years.

Why would a Bank, a College of Art, a Property Development Company and a host of others want to be involved with a homeless charity?

There are probably these three really good reasons for this; to help those less fortunate than themselves, because it's a local charity and because once you have visited and experienced the hope, positivity and change in people, it becomes infectious and you want and need to do more.

There is no explaining it.  Could it be the smiles or the proud faces of someone receiving their in-house diploma, or is it the peace showing through eyes that were dark and empty on first finding safety in the Crypt?

It could be the kindness and courteousness that is prevalent around the building or quite simply it's because we do what it says on the tin - offer a place of refuge, safety, inspiration, trust and hope for the future with love in abundance thrown in for good measure.

Something quite radical in this age of political correctness and policy regimentation.

The Crypt also takes some pride in being grateful to their partners and nurtures the relationship to ensure everyone gets the best experience or indeed value for money.

From opera to theatre to music through art and dance running alongside businesses, churches, supermarkets; the list is exhaustive and diverse.

Donations are very important to us.

The whole city mucks in and lends a hand and the Crypt shows its gratitude through its continued hard work and dedication to those most in need.

The Crypt integrates corporate teams with residents and other volunteers to ensure projects are shared and have value; that people mix and see that we are all people, we have the same concerns, woes, wants and needs.

In this way they develop a broader empathy across the city, and an empathy that should be mimicked and rebranded further afield. This creates new and vibrant partnerships, sprouting from the main root.

The Crypt strives to keep in close contact with their partners, sharing the news as it happens via social media, newsletters and events.

These are fun and interactive, providing a relaxed and warm environment for people to let their hair down, and discover and interact with the extended Crypt family. We are stronger together, whilst apart we fall.

They also encourage a feeling of worth through what's been done, and how it links into a positive outcome for residents and service users. It has to have purpose and a value for others. Otherwise what's the point?

Our busy kitchen serves 32,000 meals per year.

We're endeavouring to keep current by developing Community Interest Companies which benefit Leeds by providing employment and independence. The Crypt provides a dynamic environment to allow these partnerships to flourish and thrive.

We also have a very experimental approach with arts and cultural activities, offering a more rounded and inclusive approach to learning, whilst ensuring that the needs of the individual are at the centre of all activities.

Throughout our 85 year history, the Crypt has had to rely on partnerships, firstly with the congregation of St George's Church, then with the wider city and now with many individuals, schools, companies and centres of learning.

There really is a strength in numbers, a strength in mutual respect, a strength in mutual understanding and a respect in a shared common goal.

This is to be there for anyone in need, be a beacon of hope and a place of refuge in the storm of life.

Qari Asim outside the Makkah Masjid.

Bobby and Minal Patel from Prashad.

We work with people from all faiths and backgrounds.

Men's health day with Leeds Beckett University.

Leeds Beckett University and NHS staff with St George's Crypt and clients.

Cellist Matthew Sharp from Opera North performing a concert in the Assisi Café.

This is Nicholas.

Do you go to see Opera North?

I'm in it. I'm in Opera North and do the singing.

So you join in with it? What do you get out of joining in with Opera North?

You get to meet people and I get to enjoy myself.

What do you like about the singing? What do you like about the things that you do?

It makes me come out of my comfort zone and I enjoy doing all different stuff.

So do you feel that it brings you out of your shell a little bit?

Yes.

Do you feel confident coming out of your comfort zone?

Yes.

So how long have you been involved with Opera North?

I think either November or October – one of them.

Alright, so a fair few months.

It was in 2013, I think.

Ah right so a year and a bit?

Yeah.

What sort of music do you sing?

All different music. Starts from like 'Rest Your Weary Head' and 'Wade in the Water' and all them. All different ones. 'Make Me Feel Your Love' – I know that.

What's your favourite type of music that you sing?

I like them all.

Are you planning on staying in collaboration with Opera North?

Yes.

Where do you see the partnership going in the future? What are your ambitions with Opera North?

I'd like to come out a bit more and sing. Off my own back. Do that yeah.

So you're wanting to build your confidence a little bit more.

A bit more yeah.

Meet new people and networking?

Yeah.

Right, well I can't think of any other questions to ask. Have you got any questions?

I do another thing here as well, the Urban Sprawl. I do both of them – Opera North and Urban Sprawl.

What do Urban Sprawl do?

Singing, acting. Can't think of much else but I do the singing and the acting.

Have you been in any of the shows that they've hosted?

Yeah, I'm in them as well.

That's fine. Is there anything else you'd like to add?

No, think that's it. Far as I know. Far as I can remember anyway.

That's brilliant. Thank you very much.

Who knows where this new partnership with Suma will go?

Opera North 'SwitchON.'

An Urban Sprawl performance.

# SUCCESS

## What do we see as success?

The big house, the fast car? Maybe a successful marriage, 2.4 children? Or is it lots of money, the ability to travel where we like, eat what we like, shop where we like and wear the latest fashions?

And where in this commercially driven world do the not-haves fit? It all costs money, it all demands greed

We must all blithely follow the latest fashions and fads, but where does that leave those who cannot?

How does it feel when you can't buy the latest this or eat the latest that?

Society demands a very subjective form of success, a linear path for ambition, a meritocracy-based upon economic selfishness that all will be provided to those that deserve and that success is fair. It's balanced as long as one is willing to work. Failure is completely down to his or her actions.

It is easier to turn a blind eye to the failings of our society and gauge everything by the level that we are at.

But in that world we are all monkeys when compared with Einstein. We are all weaklings in a strong man competition. We all stink to the person with sensitive smell. We are all poor in Buckingham Palace.

And so once again what is success?

And all these measures, all these merits fail to take into account any human, emotional or moral response.

Is there success in saving lives or in loving your neighbour? In helping the person broken at the side of the road?

If there is, how is this success measured and do you think that this success ranks as highly as the financial dimension?

Is it better to stop someone from jumping or drive past unaware, sealing the next deal on your smart phone?

St George's Crypt provides a refreshing change to the busy wind of convention, the drive for more in a finite world that is steadily getting smaller.

Success in the Crypt is not marked by the speed of your motor, the size and number of rooms in your house or the five foreign holidays a year.

Success is people.

Success is supporting people to wear socks, wear shoes and brush their teeth. Success is leading someone to training and engagement activities that range from opera singing to catering.

Success is hearing that someone is happy about the activity they have done, the painting they have created.
It could also be that their family will be proud of them for engaging, that they are trying to turn their lives around.

And note there... that they are trying; they may not succeed, they may fall down and have to go back to the beginning. But in this snakes and ladders life, the Crypt never gives up.

The organisation has grown, since its creation 85 years ago, into a charity that meets the physical needs of its clients in the first instance, with a more holistic and rounded approach to help them move on.

It is all well and good to successfully house an individual, but what if they cannot cook or clean?

What if they don't have the confidence to leave that house, or when they do leave it, they fall back into old routines and lose their tenancy ending back at the Crypt door?

The Crypt has organically grown to challenge these 'failures' in its strategy, to try and help its clients to have as great a chance of success in whatever way it might present itself.

Success can be any achievement. It is just that as a society, we attribute certain achievements as worthwhile and we diminish the worth of others, marginalising people not able to interact with the social norm of success.

And so is success the clients that come through the doors on a daily basis, or organisational success?

The Crypt is bigger; more staff, greater turnover, more departments, managers, volunteers.

Nurture Catering preparing for a buffet.

More events, more supporters, a glossy newsletter.

In the corporate world, this kind of success is laudable. Who doesn't want a growing business, successful outcomes, more clients, more tweets and more friends on Facebook?

And the Crypt does not complain, going steadily about its business, trying to make successes of the clients it supports, taking up the slack and offering a wider range of services to meet the need of a growing population.

But the success of the organisation belies a more onerous underlying fact; we as a society have not ended poverty or ended homelessness, or the marginalisation of the vulnerable. Where is the success in that?

We have never been richer, never had so much, we live in a world where food is wasted on an ever increasing scale to satisfy our ever increasing demands. Strawberries in winter, spices from across the globe, rare meats cured and yet this illness persists.

The still small voice of calm. People who have lived brutal lives, unbearable abuse normalised by its immediacy and continuity find the peace to regroup, to think, to breathe; access to support is quick and easy with experts on hand to guide through the minefield of paperwork and get people engaging.

The rhetoric is the same whichever way you look at it; St George's Crypt is tangibly helping people fix their lives.

The 85 years have given a wealth of experience in how to help someone develop, to make the first steps, to support those first steps and turn them into a second. To watch, to know when to give space and when to hold, or to be close and provide a shoulder.

Every day a little miracle seems to occur, every day someone takes a step in the right direction, every day a medley of success.

As with walking, it's not always one step forward; people fall, knees are grazed, people relapse.

Living such chaotic lives means that these drops seem to the outward observer a fathomless gulf, no escape from the black hole, but next week, smile on face, the individual returns. Quietly chastised with a smile and back to business.

And is that a success? What is the greatest success? Is it the flock grazing, fattened, healthy and happy, or is it the one lost lamb, the one the shepherd must find and return to the fold?

And this is St George's Crypt; we should not live in a world where charities take up the slack of human indolence.

We should not live in a world where those most vulnerable, marginalised, hidden and obscured must make use of charity to get back on track.

It should be the place of governments and society as a whole, with more long-term structures to support the have-nots back into the world. However, in the absence of this St George's Crypt and partners fill the breach.

This is not a success for society, or a success for our modern developed world, but a small success that the tide is being challenged.

A success that the people of Leeds stand against this calculated blindness, and that the vulnerable and marginalised have a place where they can go and seek out success in one of its many wondrous and varied guises.

In Loving Memory of

## James Lawrence Hibbs

1957 – 2013

> "You can't fail to be moved by the people surrounding St George's Crypt. It represents the very best that humanity has to offer, to those who have often received the absolute worst. It has been a privilege to hear and now tell their stories."

# AUTHORS

Martell Baines

Edward Ryder

A couple of years ago I bought a copy of Entertaining Angels (the first book about St George's).

I found the story and imagery incredibly moving, and it started me thinking... 'what could I do to help?'

After chatting with Chris Fields, CEO at the Crypt, it became apparent that St George's was a very special place.

Although many changes have been made at the Crypt over the years, some aspects remain the same. Compassion, care, faith and a 'we will always help you' attitude are the same today as they were 85 years ago. Society has changed however, and not always for the best.

There are so many elements to the Crypt and the issues surrounding homelessness, that I felt we needed imagery and copy from many different sources.

In creating Entertaining More Angels, we have worked with the students and staff at Leeds College of Art. Their ideas, energy, dedication and sympathetic understanding of the key issues around the Crypt and homelessness has been truly inspiring.

What are my reasons to be involved in 'More Angels'? I think homelessness is closer to all of us than we might realise.

In searching for my reasons why I wanted to be part of the St George's Crypt Book project, I find myself returning back to someone who I knew until recently. He was an erudite gentleman, quiet and reserved. He was very much his own person and kept himself to himself. I can still recall his love of reading and the aroma of his black cherry flavoured tobacco.

When he was conversational, which became fairly rare later on, he would recount amazing stories of his travels and exploration.

We began to suspect that he might be without a home and we did not know of any family. It turned out he was stopping over some nights in the club hut and camping at other times. This is despite him having a regular job.

Then he unaccountably vanished. We had not seen him for a couple of weeks. The suspicion of him being without an address deepened into reality.

Many phone calls to hostels for the homeless, the Salvation Army, the police and reporting a missing person drew a blank. The policeman on the phone, in reassurance, said that no unaccounted for deaths had happened in the area recently.

A few days later the employer phoned back to say our missing friend had been admitted to hospital, where he had been operated on for the late stages of cancer of the throat.

The emergency services had been called by a couple at the campsite where he was found, unable to raise a call for help. He survived for a period longer and he was provided sheltered accommodation and was cared for at the end in a hospice.

At his funeral, in a full chapel with standing room only, we all stood as one to sing 'Wild Mountain Thyme' for him. He is still very much with us when we all sing it up now of an evening by Fell Beck.

Monica Merino

Working on this publication with St George's Crypt has been an emotional Journey.

To me this project was a chance to learn and collaborate with different people on something that could have a large impact on our society. Homelessness is a real issue globally, not just in Leeds. However, it is a subject full of misconceptions and assumptions, I know this because of this project.

The stories in this book have changed how I approach the word homeless and how I react when this subject comes up in a conversation. Here at the Crypt I have had the chance to meet wonderful, kind people who have extremely important stories to tell.

I have loved being a part of this publication and having a chance to shape this book into a powerful message.

George Addy

Catherine Morgan

The reason why I wanted to get involved in this project is because my final major university project was a street photography project where I interviewed elderly women on the street and took their photograph.

I thought maybe I could involve the Crypt and my project together but instead I kept them separate which was a good idea.

In February, I interviewed and then photographed several people in the Crypt which was a real eye opener for me.

These were just normal people but unfortunately life wasn't always easy.

It has been good to get involved and it makes me feel better about myself that I can document their story, because they are there to be shared and to spread awareness.

The Crypt has inspired me to help people in need, helped me with my final major project in the direction I wanted to go in and be confident in asking people questions.

When people look at this book they should think about what they could change in their lives too, even if they are not completely content with themselves.

Before visiting the crypt I had a brief idea what it might entail: soup, tea, blankets.

I was totally wrong.

I wanted to be a part of the book because the Crypt throws aside any preconceptions or judgement, only to provide genuine help and guidance to those who need it

Joe Hawkins

Rebecca Hickman

I really didn't know what to expect from the Crypt or the people within, but it's been a really fascinating experience to be part of.

Both the people that I've worked with on the project, and the clients of the Crypt, have been really great people. Meeting them and hearing their stories has opened my eyes.

In a way, the whole experience has changed my perspective on life. It's not about the material things you have, it's the memories that you make and the people around you, they're the important things. Belongings come and go.

St George's Crypt is a really impressive organisation. I have to admit that I approached it not expecting too much, but I can't believe the difference it genuinely makes to people's lives.

Their attitude of giving everyone a chance is something that's not seen enough in the world and I think everyone could benefit from adopting the way the Crypt uses this approach.

I'm extremely proud to have been a part in the creation of the book, and to tell more people about the work that goes on in this charity.

I have thoroughly enjoyed working with St George's Crypt in the process of making this book.

The project has opened my eyes to the support network that is on offer to the disadvantaged people of Leeds.

Being a photographer in the project has given me a chance to meet some of people that use the facilities and services of the Crypt and talk to them about how it has helped... or is helping them become a better person.

Andrew Omond

I met Ed at a Common Purpose function. Whilst chatting about what we did, he showed interest in our work and was really excited about getting involved. We talked through the possibilities and he said that he had been inspired by our first book and would really like to help bring it up to date.

Now the process is over and the new book is coming to completion. The effort of everyone involved is plain to see; it is a testament to Ed that he has persevered, held the group together and given us this wonderful tool to showcase the work we do here, and how we have developed and grown that work over the past 85 years.

'Long may it continue!'

Ailsa Read

Sharon Heleine

My experience working with St George's Crypt has been very enlightening, although I have known the Crypt for many years, having lived and worked in Leeds all my life.

I was so surprised at the happiness and laughter in the Crypt. Everyone chatted and was so welcoming. Lots of smiling and shaking hands goes on!

The other surprise for me was the multi-faith interaction, from all the religions in Leeds which pull together in providing help and food, even though this was basically a Christian foundation, that was wonderful and an example to the world.

The Chaplin, Roger Quick, is an inspiration.

Altogether, a wonderful positive experience meeting and chatting to both the clients and the helpers.

I hope this book will help to raise both money and also an awareness of the work by the dedicated team at the Crypt.

I have admired the St George's Crypt team for years, and I became involved in Entertaining More Angels via my work at Leeds College of Art.

One of the qualities I admire the most, is the patience, tolerance and non-judgemental attitude of staff and volunteers.

All of them could choose to work somewhere easier, where the results are more tangible, where problems are more solvable, where the pay is higher, where the future is less precarious and yet they stay.

While most of us are focused on enjoying material success and quality time with family and friends, the St George's Crypt crew have decided to help others rather than themselves.

And show me another CEO at work at 6am every day making everyone soup for lunch.

It's been a delight to work with the six Leeds College of Art students who have contributed photographs, illustrations and interviews.

They have challenged our acceptance of the status quo, asking why St George's Crypt is still needed in one of the world's richest economies, why society is hypocritical about standards of behaviour and why people buy themselves luxuries when they could donate money to change lives.

It's been a privilege to be on the team.

# FUTURE

St George's Crypt has always remained true to its founding principles of Christian belief and the unconditional offering of care and support to people in need.

In order to best achieve these principles, it has developed and strengthened the range of services provided and, crucially, the manner in which these services are delivered.

The levels of professionalism of staff and trustees have kept pace with the requirements of legislation, good practice and key skill sets.

This has enabled the Crypt to develop and deepen relationships and partnerships with the corporate sector, the public sector and a wide range of donors from many walks of life.

There have been major strides in the standard of accommodation offered, and also in consciously seeking to provide the clients with real opportunities to learn new skills and to grow in self-confidence.

This in turn leads to placements in the Crypt and eventually to real jobs in the charity. It is a real joy to be able to state that 20% of Crypt staff are former clients or ex-offenders.

85 years on, there are fresh challenges which are now being met by the Crypt.

The period of austerity has resulted in a climate in which public sector funding is under increased scrutiny. Many corporate supporters are looking closely at charitable giving to make sure they can demonstrate best value for money.

Charitable trusts have less disposable income due to record low interest rates, and individuals are reviewing their charitable donations in many cases.

The Crypt remains confident that it can adapt and respond.

New income streams have been created through the development of the retail businesses, and plans are afoot to develop housing units which will benefit both Crypt clients and also people in need from council lists.

The charity does offer a range of services which is unrivalled in Leeds.

Many clients express their gratitude for the non-judgemental approach and also the empathetic methods of the staff.

It is vital to continue to review and revisit business strategies, but always to remember that at the heart of the Crypt is the client.

The Crypt's history demonstrates throughout a commitment to adaptation, ingenuity and responsiveness to new challenges.

It is hard to say that St George's Crypt will be here in 85 years' time, but it would be wrong to bet against it.

There is a remarkable resilience which has run through the Crypt for the first 85 years and fortifies the charity for future challenges.

The Church is in need of good models of social action and mission.

St George's Crypt was first inspired by the example of Revd. Dick Shepherd who founded a Crypt at St Martin in the Fields.

It is to be hoped that the resilience and proven success of working with people with increasingly complex issues, and who face massive challenges in everyday life can inspire others to learn from our experience.

The Church has so much to offer people in need today – more than ever!

# NOW WHAT?

# Thank you for reading Entertaining More Angels.

We hope it demonstrates the beacon of light and hope that St George's Crypt represents to homeless and vulnerable people in Leeds.

Many people may have heard the name but may not know exactly what the Crypt provides, nor how to help.

Did you know in 2014 the Crypt helped 1,022 people who would otherwise have been street homeless? We also served over 32,000 meals that year too.

At any one time, we can provide 27 warm beds on bitterly cold nights and endless cups of hot steaming tea and coffee.

There is a running joke that the Crypt can never have too much tea, coffee, sugar and washing powder!

The Crypt may have started out as a soup kitchen of sorts, but over the course of 85 years we have evolved beyond recognition, now encompassing two charity shops, two cafés and a canteen.

We are the only charity in Leeds to have a wet and dry hostel and plans are afoot to provide 20 homes.

We have an extensive training and engagement programme geared towards instilling vital skills in our clients such as literacy and numeracy, through to managing personal finances and learning basic First Aid or studying for NVQs.

We also liaise with the Department for Work and Pensions to help get people job ready, and provide physiotherapy to soothe away aches and pains.

However, all work and no play makes Jack a dull boy! Lots of fun things occur too.

We have excellent relationships with Opera North and Urban Sprawl who help bolster client self–esteem and confidence through music and drama.

To help spread the word (and work) of the Crypt, in one year we gave 76 talks and conducted 102 tours.

Unfortunately, being a beacon of light and hope does not come free.

As of 2014, it costs the Crypt £28,000 a week or £1.5 million per year to provide the services that are so instrumental in changing peoples' lives for the better.

However, there are many ways that you can support St George's Crypt; offering your time, skills and experience as a volunteer, donating food or goods, or by making a financial gift.

People forget that we have to pay the bills, and bills for over 1,000 people don't come cheap!

# WHAT'S £2?

A quick
coffee

or

A three
course meal
at the crypt

# HOW CAN YOU HELP?

## WAYS TO GIVE

**CHEQUE** - Post a cheque made payable to St George's Crypt.

**DEBIT/CREDIT CARD** - Card donations can be made using the donate button on our website www.stgeorgescrypt.org.uk

**ONLINE** - Use the Local Giving website: https://localgiving.com/charity/stgeorgescrypt

**STANDING ORDER** - Print out a standing order form from our website, or contact us with your details to receive a form by mail.

**DIRECT FROM YOUR ACCOUNT** - Our bank account details for receiving donations are:

HSBC; sort code 40-27-15; account number 54703537.

Please contact our fundraising department to inform us if you donate directly from your bank so we can make a proper record of your donation.

**PAYPAL** - Use the donate button on our website: www.stgeorgescrypt.org.uk to make a contribution from your PayPal account.

**CASH** - If you are unable to donate using any of these methods and wish to donate cash, please visit our centre during office hours. Please do not send cash through the post.

**LEAVE A GIFT IN YOUR WILL** - Make a bequest in your Will to leave a lasting legacy supporting the homeless. We cannot provide legal advice, but our fundraising team will help with further information if required.

**GIFTS IN MEMORY** - Commemorate the life of a loved one by donating to St George's Crypt in their memory. Contact us if you would like gift aid envelopes.

**ORGANISE OR TAKE PART IN A CRYPT FOCUSED EVENT** - Ask for fundraising ideas - a fundraising pack. Use 'Just Giving' to take the hassle out of collecting sponsorship.

**VOLUNTEER** - If you would like to volunteer, you can contact our volunteer coordinator via email: volunteer@stgeorgescrypt.org.uk

**If you have any questions about making a donation to St George's Crypt, please contact us on: 0113 245 9061 or email: fundraising1@stgeorgescrypt.org.uk**

Run for All Leeds 10k participants raising money for the Crypt.

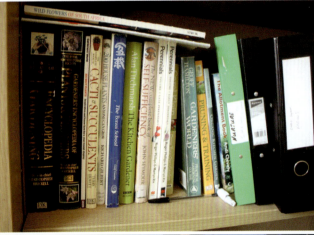

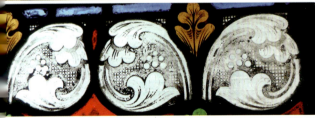

FRIENDS